The Essential Guide to Writing Research Papers

The Essential Guide to Writing Research Papers

Canadian Edition

James D. Lester
Austin Peay State University

James D. Lester, Jr.
Clayton College and State University

Patricia I. Mochnacz
University of Manitoba

Longman

Toronto

To my family

National Library of Canada Cataloguing in Publication Data

Lester, James D., 1935–
   The essential guide to writing research papers

Canadian ed.
Includes index.
ISBN 0-321-11513-9

1. Report writing. I. Lester, James D., 1959- II. Mochnacz, Patricia
I., 1943- III. Title.

LB2369.L49 2002   808.02   C2002-900006-8

ISBN 0-321-11513-9

Vice President, Editorial Director: Michael J. Young
Acquisitions Editor: Marianne Minaker
Signing Representative: Duncan MacKinnon
Developmental Editor: Craig Pyette
Marketing Manager: Toivo Pajo
Production Editor: Cheryl Jackson
Copy Editor: Ann McInnis
Proofreader: Marie Graham
Production Coordinator: Peggy Brown
Page Layout: Jansom
Art Director: Julia Hall
Cover Design: Amy Harnden

5   07 06 05

Printed and bound in Canada

Contents

Chapter 3   SEARCHING THE WORLD WIDE WEB   19

Chapter 4   COLLECTING DATA OUTSIDE THE LIBRARY   31

Chapter 5   ORGANIZING IDEAS AND SETTING GOALS   35

Chapter 8   DRAFTING THE PAPER IN AN ACADEMIC STYLE   69

Chapter 9   USING MLA STYLE   86

Chapter 10 USING APA STYLE   118

Chapter 11 USING THE CBE STYLES FOR SCIENTIFIC PAPERS 138

Chapter 12 USING THE CMS (CHICAGO) NOTE STYLE 149

Preface

*T*he *Essential Guide to Writing Research Papers,* Canadian Edition, is designed for students in both in first year and upper level courses in all disciplines. As in its previous editions, the text makes the fundamentals of research paper writing accessible in a brief, handy format, but this edition also features extensive coverage of electronic research. It remains rooted in the fundamentals of thorough library research, but encourages both Internet and field research. It carries you from the discovery of a topic to research to note taking, writing, and formatting the finished manuscript to a specific style. Trustworthy guidelines and advice are illustrated with helpful examples taken from various disciplines and explanations when necessary. The convenient size and design make *The Essential Guide* an ideal reference for research writing throughout a university or college career.

New Emphasis on Canadian Content

Canada's broad cultural and ethnic diversity is reflected in references to the Asian Canadian people of British Columbia in Joy Kogawa's *Obasan,* the small town prairie people of Margaret Laurence's "Manawaka," the Québecoises of Michel Tremblay's *Les belles-soeurs,* and the Aboriginal women of Tomson Highway's *The Rez Sisters.* References to Canadian history include icons such as Nellie McClung and Pierre Trudeau; historical events mentioned in the text include the October Crisis of 1970, the birth of Canada's newest territory (Nunavut), and Canada's role as peacekeeper in the 21st century.

To facilitate the process of researching, we've made reference to Canadian bibliographies and websites from across the disciplines, such as: *Bibliography of Theatre History in Canada, Canadian History: A Reader's Guide,* and *The Annotated Bibliography of Canada's Major Authors,* as well as the Canadian Astronomical Websites, Canadian Government Information on the Internet (CGII), Health Canada Online, and Early Canadiana Online.

New Emphasis on Writing in the Disciplines

This text explores research, style, and format through the lenses of many disciplines, helping students in the humanities, social sciences, and natural sciences to approach a topic in a given field, conduct valid research, and present the results in an appropriate format. The Canadian edition of the text therefore includes the following:

- Comprehensive lists of discipline-specific scholarly bibliographies and printed indexes.
- Comprehensive lists of websites and search engines from across the disciplines.
- Continued coverage, with sample student papers, of **MLA** and **CMS (Chicago)** documentation styles.
- Increased coverage of **APA** documentation style.
- Coverage of *both* the **citation–sequence** system and the **name-year** system for students using the **CBE** documentation styles for scientific papers.

New Coverage of Electronic Research Tools

A new chapter—Chapter 3, "Searching the World Wide Web"—offers advice on using every aspect of the Internet, including subject-directory, robot-driven, and metasearch search engines, Internet bibliographies, and discipline-specific search engines. This new chapter also provides advice for finding useful home pages, online magazines, and news articles; using listserv, usenet, and chat; and evaluating Internet sources.

New Coverage of Field Research

A new chapter—Chapter 4, "Collecting Data Outside the Library"—guides students in finding their own primary sources, from reading personal papers and setting up interviews to using media sources, as well as conducting research using questionnaires, case studies, observation, and laboratory tests.

Continued Coverage of the Ethical Dimensions of Research

Continued emphasis on the ethics of research focuses on such issues as crediting online sources and avoiding plagiarism.

Website

The Companion Website at **www.ablongman.awl.com/lester** provides activities specific to each chapter's content, such as using keywords to find and narrow a topic, using listserv archives as potential research areas, and evaluating different kinds of Web materials.

Acknowledgments

I wish to thank the following people for their assistance in developing the Canadian edition of this text: Marlene Milne for her insightful suggestions; Associate Editor Craig Pyette for his valuable assistance, support, and sense of humour; Mary Ann Steggles, University of Manitoba, for encouraging her students to submit papers to me; Barbara Rudyk, University of Manitoba, for her constant support and encouragement; and especially Christine Butterill, University of Manitoba, for her valuable contribution to the sections on writing notes and avoiding plagiarism in Chapters 6 and 7, her meticulous attention to detail as she edited the manuscript, and her unceasing encouragement and faith in my ability to bring this work to fruition.

My gratitude also goes to the many University of Manitoba students who submitted their work for consideration as sample papers, and especially to the following students, who generously allowed me to adapt their papers for this text:

Jennifer Kroetsch for "Canadian Regulation of Herbal Remedies" in Chapter 11.

Katrina A. T. Senyk for "Breaking the Mould: Artemisia's Contribution to Art" in Chapters 9 and 12.

Jennifer Sinclair for "The Exhaustion of Canada's Human Resources" in Chapter 6.

C. Turenne for "Aboriginal Education in Canada: A Work in Progress" in Chapter 10.

Lastly, I wish to express my love for, and gratitude to my husband, Don, and my family, whose love and support made my foray into the world of authorship possible.

Patricia I. Mochnacz

1 Finding a Scholarly Topic

As you move from class to class and from instructor to instructor you will find that in some courses you are free to choose a research topic that interests you, in others you must select a topic closely related to the content of the course, and in still others a specific topic will be assigned. The first step in writing a research paper is to find a workable topic that fulfills the requirements of the assignment and that adopts a serious scholarly perspective. The research project begins when you select a general subject and an issue that interests you:

current events (effects of maternal smoking)
education (standardized testing in public schools)
family issues (parents who lie to their children)
science (genetic engineering and cloning)

In particular, try to select a topic that will (1) examine a significant issue, (2) advance the reader's knowledge, and (3) display a serious purpose that demands analysis of the issues, argues from a position, and explains complex details.

You need not abandon a favourite topic, such as "Fishing in Lake Winnipeg." Just be certain to give it a serious, scholarly perspective: "The Effects of Toxic Chemicals on the Fish of Lake Winnipeg." When your topic addresses a problem or raises an issue, you have a reason to

- examine specific sources in the library
- share your scholarship with the reader
- write a meaningful conclusion

Start by generating your own ideas (see 1a). If that does not produce a good topic, you may wish to search electronic sources (see 1b). The library's printed sources may also suggest a topic (see 1c).

Hint: Topic selection goes beyond choosing a general category (e.g., Canada as peacekeeper); it includes finding a research-provoking issue (e.g., Canada's role as peacekeeper should be increased in the 21st century). That is, as a researcher you need to take a stand and adopt a belief.

1a Generating Your Own Ideas for a Research Topic

1a

Ideas for a research paper can be generated by several activities.

Using Personal Experience

Everyone has special interests. One of three techniques can spark your interest and perhaps help you discover a writing topic:

1. Combine a personal interest with some aspect of your academic studies: "Skiing and Sports Medicine" or "Video Games and Mathematics."
2. Consider career interests: a business student might develop the topic "Student Credit Cards and Interest Rates," but a chemistry student might prefer "Rural Water Tables and the Invasion of Chemical Toxins."
3. Let your cultural background prompt you toward detailed research into your roots, your culture, and the mythology and history of your ethnic background, such as "The Role of Aboriginal People in the Founding of Canada" or "The Migration of Scottish Children to the Maritime Provinces." These are general subjects that you can narrow later to a specific issue.

Talking with Others

Consult with your instructor, fellow students, family members, specialists on the Internet, and experts in books and articles. As you share your thoughts with others, something said might refine your ideas for a good topic. For example, one writer discovered her topic by observing her mother, who had become addicted to the Internet. The writer seized upon the idea, researched it carefully, talked with her mother, and produced a paper entitled "Internet Addiction: The Destruction of a Family."

> ***Hint:*** Casual conversations that contribute to your understanding of the subject do not need to be documented. However, a formal interview or an in-depth discussion with an expert will demand credit in your text and a citation in the bibliography at the end of your research project.

Free Writing and Brainstorming

Free writing is an exercise that requires non-stop writing for a page or so to develop valuable phrases, comparisons, personal anecdotes, and specific thoughts that help focus issues of concern. Note this brief example that starts to explore this writer's concerns about the topic:

Tabloid television seems to me a good name for what has been happening with television talk shows. These shows just sensationalize the personal, private misery of many people. How often have I wondered, "Is this really true?" It seems like people will say or do just about anything to appear on TV.

Brainstorm! Make a list of key words (in any order) for fundamental terms and concepts that might focus the direction of your research. One student listed several terms and phrases about the structure of Canada's government:

Federal	Governor General	Senate
Role of the Monarch	House of Commons	Democracy
Municipal Government	Provincial Legislatures	Constitution
Prime Minister	Cabinet	

She arranged the key words into a **rough outline** to find the hierarchy of major and minor issues, a ranking that would mature during her research.

The Structure of Canadian Government

Federal State	Parliamentary Democracy	The Monarchy
Federal Parliament	Senate	Governor General
Provincial Legislatures	House of Commons	Constitution
Municipal Governments	Prime Minister and Cabinet	

Keep a **research journal** to record ideas arising from your free writing and brainstorming, as well as notes or questions on specific issues related to your subject.

1b Using Electronic Sources to Discover a Good Topic

Several types of electronic sources provide ways to investigate a subject for its potential as a scholarly topic.

Using the World Wide Web

The **Internet** is a worldwide computer network that consists of millions of computers and computer files that form a huge library of source materials. At the beginning of your research, read some of the articles at Internet sites to see what others are saying on the topic. You might find a good idea for your own research. In accessing this network, most researchers now use the **World Wide Web**.

If you need a subject, use a subject directory to move from a general subject to a specific topic. The subject directories on search engines such as *AltaVista* or *Yahoo!* are hierarchical; with each mouse click you narrow the topic to a more specific subject (e.g., from Health to Disease to Diabetes). See pp. 19–26 for more information on subject directories.

Many of these same sites allow **keyword searches.** These searches reveal addresses and descriptions of websites that use your keywords. The results of a keyword search can tell you if a topic has been researched by others. For example, entering *October Crisis 1970* and *Pierre Trudeau* will direct you to sites (URLs) where you can begin reading: **www.clevernet.on.ca/pierre_trudeau/links_pierre_trudeau.html** or **www.cbc.ca/millennium/timelines/feature_octobercrisis.html**. (See also 3a, pages 19–21.)

For detailed information on searching the World Wide Web, see Chapter 3.

1c

Using a Library's Electronic Databases

Most college and university libraries now have electronic databases, such as *InfoTrac, EBSCOhost, Silverplatter,* or *UMI-ProQuest.* These database files refer you to thousands of magazine and journal articles, many of which are peer reviewed by experts in the academic field. In many cases you can read an abstract of the article and, on occasion, print the entire article. These more scholarly articles let you know what others are writing on your subject and help you to focus your topic. Libraries will vary in their database holdings, so it is important for you to develop a working relationship with the reference librarians. For more information on researching these databases, see pages 14–16.

Using CD-ROMs

Browsing through CD-ROMs, such as *The Canadian Encyclopedia; For Seven Generations: An Information Legacy of the Royal Commission on Aboriginal Peoples; Encarta;* or *Electronic Classical Library,* will give you a good feel for the subject and suggest a list of narrowed topics. Also, CD-ROMs may be available in a specialty area, such as *Roget's Thesaurus of English Words and Phrases, IBM Dictionary of Computing,* or *World Shakespeare Bibliography on CD-ROM.*

Using the Electronic Catalogue to Find a Topic

Most university, college, and public libraries now have an electronic catalogue, which is a computer version of the card catalogue. This catalogue has different names at different libraries, for example, INFOGATE at UBC, BISON at the University of Manitoba, ORBIS at the University of Ottawa, Quest at the University of New Brunswick. It primarily indexes books, journals and other materials, but not articles in magazines and journals. Like the CD-ROM databases, it will help you find a topic by guiding you quickly from general subjects to subtopics and finally to specific books. See Chapter 2, pages 11–14 for more information on how to use the electronic book catalogue.

1c Using Printed Sources to Formulate a Topic

As with Internet sources, look to see how your topic is being talked about in the literature. Carefully read the **titles** of books and articles and make a record of key terminology. For example, the title "Television Literacy for Gifted Children" provides two possible subjects for a research paper: *television literacy* and *gifted children.*

Inspect a book's **table of contents** to find a subject that interests you. A history book dealing with Canada's role as a peacekeeper might display these headings in its table of contents:

The Cold War
Keeping the Peace
The Former Yugoslavia
Cambodia
Somalia

If any of these headings look interesting, go to the book's **index** or the **subheadings** in the table of contents for additional areas of interest, such as this example:

> The Former Yugoslavia
> > Canadians in Croatia, 122–123
> > A Visit to Sarajevo: General A. J. G. D. de Chastelain, 124–128
> > Casualties, 129
> > The Medak Pocket: Canada's Biggest Battle Since Korea, 136–147

If you see something that looks interesting, the logical follow-up involves reading the designated pages to consider issues and to find a general subject for your work. For example, the list above might suggest a student's investigation of why the incident at Medak developed so quickly into a full-scale military operation.

Searching the Headings in the Printed Indexes

Any major index collection in the library's reference section, such as the *Readers' Guide to Periodical Literature, Bibliographic Index,* or *Humanities Index,* categorizes and subdivides topics in alphabetical order. Searching under a key word or phrase will usually locate a list of critical articles on a subject. Studying the titles of these articles might suggest a good topic. For example, by looking for information on suffrage in Canada in the *Readers' Guide to Periodical Literature*, a researcher would find the following article, cited here in MLA style:

> Taylor, Rupert J. "A Battle Not Yet Won." <u>Canada and the World
> > Backgrounder</u> 60 (1995): 4–7.

This search would also lead the researcher to 10 other articles in a special issue of this journal devoted to women's issues.

1d Narrowing the Topic

Generating your own ideas and searching electronic and printed sources will lead to a general topic or issue that interests you; the next step is to narrow this topic.

Asking questions that focus your attention on primary issues will help you frame a workable topic that is neither too broad nor too narrow. Ask yourself questions that force you to define the terminology and address the issues. For example, after reading about Canada's military involvement in the former Yugoslavia, one writer asked: What is "peacekeeping"? Is it effective? Should Canada adopt the global role of peacekeeper?

Asking questions can help you to narrow the topic and ultimately to formulate a working thesis statement, such as: "Canada's role as peacekeeper should be expanded in the 21st century."

1e Writing the Thesis Statement

1e

One sentence in the introduction to your paper should express the controlling ideas for the entire paper. This sentence, called the thesis statement, makes an assertion that you will examine in your research and explain in your paper. The thesis statement should normally be placed at the end of your introduction.

A thesis statement expands your topic into a scholarly proposal that you will try to prove and defend in your paper. Do not state the obvious: "Too much television is harmful to children." Instead, find a critical focus: "Violence in children's programming echoes a young person's fascination with brutality." The working thesis advances an idea that the writer expects to develop fully and defend with the evidence. It may change as the work continues. Meanwhile, the thesis makes a connection between the subject, *television violence,* and the focusing agent, *adolescent behaviour.*

Accordingly, a writer's critical approach to the subject affects the thesis. One writer's social concern for battered wives will generate a different thesis statement than another person's biological approach:

SOCIAL APPROACH   Public support of "safe" houses for battered wives seems to be a public endorsement of divorce.

BIOLOGICAL APPROACH   Battered wives may be the victims of their own biological conditioning.

The two thesis statements shown above will provoke a response from the reader, who will demand a carefully structured defence in the body of the paper.

Your thesis is not your conclusion or your answer to a problem. Rather, the thesis anticipates your conclusion. It sets in motion the examination of facts and points the reader toward the special ideas of your paper, which you will save for the conclusion.

Avoiding False Assumptions

Be careful to avoid false assumptions in your thesis statement, as in the following example:

Some battered women accept their fate of a bad marriage because of low self-esteem.

The thesis that some women accept being battered because their low self-esteem gives them a passive, compliant nature is quite acceptable. However, the writer cannot *assume* that a battered woman is in a "bad" marriage, since this may be viewed by some as a false statement. To avoid this, restate the thesis:

Some battered women accept their fate because of low self-esteem.

In addition to the *thesis* as the controlling agent for a research paper, see also Chapter 10, page 118, which discusses the use of the *hypothesis* and the *prediction.*

1f

Using Explanation, Analysis, and Persuasion

The effective use of **explanation, analysis,** and **persuasion** will improve your writing.

1. Use *explanation* to review and itemize factual data. For example, one writer explained how advertisers have gained entrance into classrooms by providing free educational materials.
2. Use *analysis* to classify various parts of the subject and to investigate each one in depth. The same writer classified and examined the methods used by advertisers to reach schoolchildren with their messages.
3. Use *persuasion* to defend your argument convincingly. This writer then condemned the use of advertising and warned of its dangers, arguing that advertisers have enticed children into bad habits: eating improperly, smoking cigarettes, drinking alcohol, or behaving violently.

Persuasion enables you to reject the general attitudes about a problem and to affirm new theories, advance a solution, recommend a course of action, and—as mentioned above—invite the reader into an intellectual dialogue. Sometimes, however, you will be asked to submit a research paper that is informative, not persuasive, in which case you need only explain and analyze your research findings, not defend a certain position or point of view. Be sure that you know if your paper should be informative or persuasive.

Identifying Your Audience

You will want to design your research paper for an audience of interested readers who expect a depth of understanding on your part and evidence of your background reading on this special topic. You should try to say something worthwhile and new. Do not bore your readers or insult their intelligence by retelling known facts from an encyclopedia. (This latter danger is the reason many instructors discourage your use of an encyclopedia as a source.)

Identifying Your Role as a Researcher

Your paper should reflect the investigative nature of your work, so try to display your knowledge. In short, make it *your* discourse, not a collection of quotations from experts in the books and journals. Your role is to investigate, explain, defend, and argue the issue at hand, all at the same time in the same paper and with proper citations. Refer to authorities that you have consulted; do not hide them. After all, the ideas of others are of paramount interest both to you and to your readers. Offer quotations. Provide charts or graphs that you have created or copied from the sources. Your instructors will give you credit for using the sources in your paper. Just be certain that you give in-text citations to the sources to reflect your academic honesty.

1f Drafting a Research Proposal

A research proposal helps to clarify and focus the project. It comes in two forms: (1) a short paragraph to identify the project for yourself and your instructor, or (2) several pages to give background information, your rationale for conducting the study, a review of the literature, your methods, and

1f

conclusions you hope to prove. In either case, it should quickly identify four essential ingredients of your work:

a. The purpose of the paper (inform, explain, analyze, argue).
b. The intended audience (general or specialized).
c. Your position as the writer (informer, interpreter, evaluator, reviewer, or advocate).
d. The preliminary thesis statement or opening hypothesis.

Writing a Short Research Proposal

One writer developed this brief proposal:

The writer identifies the subject.	This report will deal with the issues facing parents who have children who are diagnosed with Attention Deficit Hyperactivity Disorder (ADHD). I'm one of those parents, so this study touches my life. In it, I will
She advances the hypothesis that she will evaluate.	evaluate this hypothesis: Medication is the best treatment for ADHD. Respected authorities in the field state over and over again that medication is the only known solution to the treatment of this disorder. Even
She refers to the sources.	with experts backing medication, there is still resistance to medicating children. To support my claim, I have
She indicates her plans for interviews.	planned for interviews with people who either have ADHD or have children with ADHD.

Writing a Detailed Research Proposal

A long research proposal presents specific details concerning the project:

1. A *cover page* with the title of the project, your name, and, if necessary, the person or agency to whom you are submitting the proposal.
2. An *abstract* that summarizes your project in 50 to 100 words. (See pages 15 and 132 for examples.)
3. A *purpose statement* that includes your *rationale* for the project. (See the brief proposal above for an example.)
4. A *statement of qualification* that explains your experience and perhaps the special qualities that you bring to the project. If you have no experience with the subject, you can omit the statement of qualification.
5. A *review of the literature* that surveys the articles and books you have examined in your preliminary work. (See pages 53–55 for an example of a literature review.)
6. A presentation of your research methods is a description of the design of the *materials*, your *timetable* for completing the project, and, when applicable, your *budget*.

Whether a short or long research proposal is required, it is now time to go in search of evidence that will defend the argument. This is the point at which the writer conducts research in the library (see Chapter 2); on the Internet (see Chapter 3); and in the field (see Chapter 4).

2 Library Research

The search for sources is a serious task and one that might frustrate you periodically. Some leads will turn out to be dead ends; other leads will provide only trivial information. Some research will be duplicated, and a recursive pattern will develop; that is, you will go back and forth from reading, to searching, and to reading again. One idea will modify another, you will discover connections, and a fresh perspective—your own—will emerge.

2a Steps in the Research Process

Your research strategy should include the following steps, with adjustments for individual needs:

1. Research the available sources: printed indexes, abstracts, bibliographies, and reference books, as well as electronic sources. This search should provide several benefits:

   - It gives you an overview of the subject.
   - It provides a beginning set of reference citations.
   - It allows you the chance to define and restrict the subject.
   - It suggests the availability of sufficient sources with diverse opinions.

2. Refine the topic and evaluate the sources: Spend time browsing, reading abstracts, skimming articles, comparing sources, making citation searches, and reading through pertinent sections of books. See Chapter 6 for details.
3. Read and take notes: Draw ideas and quotations from books, articles, essays, reviews, government documents, and electronic sources. See Chapter 7 for details.

Once you have decided on a topic, you can begin your research in three different places—the library, the Internet, and the field. The next three chapters explore these options. First, let's examine the library's holdings for general and discipline-specific research.

> **Hint:** Most of the printed reference works described in this chapter are available on the various databases in your library's electronic network.

2b

2b Developing a Working Bibliography

A working bibliography is a list of the sources that you plan to read before drafting your paper. Too few sources will indicate that your topic is too narrow or obscure. Too many sources will indicate that you need a tighter focus. Each working bibliography entry should contain the following information, with variations dependent on the discipline in which you are working:

1. Author's name
2. Title of the work
3. Publication information (city, publisher, year, volume number, pages, etc.)
4. Library call number (the book's "address" in the library; see page 11)
5. A personal note about the contents of the source (optional)

Write information in the style requested by your instructor or as dictated by your topic's general discipline.

MLA Style for Papers in the Humanities (Especially Language and Literature)

See Chapter 9 for full details on the style advocated by the Modern Language Association and use these basic forms for a book and a periodical article.

> Garrett-Petts, William F. <u>Writing about Literature: A Guide for the Student Critic</u>. Peterborough, ON: Broadview Press, 2000.
> Emilsson, Wilhelm. "Icelandic Voices." <u>Canadian Literature</u> 162 (1999): 231–34.

APA Style for Papers in the Social Sciences

See Chapter 10 for full details on the style advocated by the American Psychological Association and use these basic forms for a book and a periodical article.

> Ghosh, R., & Ray, D. (Eds.). (1995). *Social change and education in Canada* (3rd ed.). Toronto: Harcourt Brace, Canada.
> Johnson, E. A., & Stewart, D. W. (2000). Clinical supervision in Canadian academic and service settings: The importance of education, training, and workplace support for supervisor development. *Canadian Psychology, 41*, 124–130.

CBE Style for Papers in the Sciences

See Chapter 11 for full details on the style advocated by the Council of Science Editors (formerly the Council of Biology Editors) and use these basic forms for a book and a periodical article.

> Thadani M. Herbal remedies: Weeding fact from fiction. Winnipeg (MB): Cantext; 1999.
> Kalant H. The pharmacology and toxicology of "ecstasy" (MDMA) and related drugs. CMAJ 2001;165:917–28.

CMS (Chicago) Style for Papers in the Humanities

See Chapter 12 for full details on the style advocated by the *Chicago Manual of Style* and use these basic forms for a book and a periodical article.

> Friesen, Gerald. *River Road: Essays on Manitoba and Prairie History*. Winnipeg: University of Manitoba Press: 1996.
> Spear, Richard. "Artemisia Gentileschi: Ten Years of Fact and Fiction." *Art Bulletin* 82 (September 2000): 568–579.

2c

For other types of entries (e.g., anthology, lecture, map), consult the index, which will direct you to appropriate pages in Chapters 9, 10, 11, and 12 for samples of almost every imaginable type of bibliographic entry. Format your working bibliography in the same style you will be using in your finished paper.

Note that the *MLA Handbook for Writers of Research Papers*, 5th edition, still recommends underlining titles of works, but MLA editors have recently indicated that either underlining or italics are acceptable, and publications in the PMLA (Publication of the Modern Languages Association) use italics.

In addition, the use of underlining to represent italics becomes a problem when you compose texts for online publication. On the World Wide Web, underlining in a document indicates that the underlined word or phrase is an active hypertext link. (All HTML editing programs automatically underline any text linked to another hypertext or website.)

However, in order to adhere to the style demonstrated in the *MLA Handbook for Writers of Research Papers*, 5th edition, underlining is used in this text for all examples written according to MLA style.

Note that APA and CMS (Chicago) recommend the use of italics, while CBE style does not specify the use of either italics or underlining.

In all cases, be sure to check with your instructors as to their preferences, and see the Appendix, page 174, for information on which titles should be underlined or italicized, and which should be placed in quotation marks.

2c Finding Books on Your Topic

The library is no longer just a repository of printed materials. Much of your research will be conducted on the library's electronic network with call numbers to its own books and with links to sources around the world. Your library will classify its books by one of two systems, the Library of Congress (LC) system or the Dewey Decimal System. The next example shows the differences in the systems:

Library of Congress:		*Dewey Decimal:*	
TD	[Environmental Technology]	628.53	[Engineering & Allied operations]
833	[Air Pollution]	.H48	[Author Number]
.H461u	[Author Number]		

By using either set of numbers, depending upon your library, you would find this book, noted here in MLA Style.

> Hesketh, Howard E. <u>Understanding and Controlling Air Pollution</u>.
> 2nd ed. Ann Arbor: Ann Arbor Science, 1974.

Record the *complete* call number. Writing the correct form now will save a great deal of time when you are rushing to complete your paper.

Using the Library's Electronic Book Catalogue

Your library's computerized catalogue probably has a special name, like INFOGATE at UBC, BISON at the University of Manitoba, ORBIS at the University of Ottawa, and Quest at the University of New Brunswick. It primarily indexes books, journals and other materials, but not articles in magazines and journals. It lists these resources by call number, filed by subject, author and title. Begin your research by using a *keyword search*, such as "suffrage." You will see a list of books on the monitor, and you can click the mouse on each one to gather more information, such as the contents of the book and where to find it in the library. For example:

Keyword	suffrage
Title	International encyclopedia of women's suffrage
Author	Hannam, June

For tips on keyword searching, see Chapter 3, page 20.

Searching Online and Printed Bibliographies

A bibliography tells you what books are available for a specific subject. If you have a clearly defined topic, skip to page 13, "Searching in the Specialized Bibliographies." If you are still trying to formulate a clear focus, begin with one of the general guides to titles of books to refine your search. These guides may be accessed electronically or found on the shelves in printed versions.

Searching in General Bibliographies

There are several broad-based reference books to information on many subjects:

A Bibliography of Canadian Bibliographies
A World Bibliography of Bibliographies
Bibliographic Index: A Cumulative Bibliography of Bibliographies
Where to Find What: A Handbook to Reference Service

Figure 2.1 shows how *Bibliographic Index* will send you to bibliographic lists inside books. In this case, the bibliography will be found on pages 105–112 of Sarnoff's book.

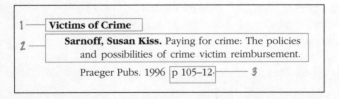

Figure 2.1: From *Bibliographic Index, 2000*: (1) subject heading, (2) entry of a book that contains a bibliography on crime, (3) specific pages on which the bibliography is located.

If this work fits your research, you would probably want to write a bibliography entry so you can examine the book's bibliography for additional articles on this topic. Here it is in MLA style:

> Sarnoff, Susan Kiss. <u>Paying for Crime: The Policies and Possibilities of Crime Victim Reimbursement</u>. New York: Praeger, 1996. Bibl on 105–12.

2c

Searching in the Specialized Bibliographies

If you have narrowed your subject, search one or two of the discipline-specific guides and bibliographies listed below. These are well-indexed references that take you to more specific books. They may be online or on the shelves. Librarians at the reference desk can help you find them.

Humanities	
Art	*Bibliographic Guide to Art and Architecture*
	Fine Arts: A Bibliographic Guide
Drama	*Bibliography of Theatre History in Canada*
	Cambridge Guide to Theatre
History	*Canadian History: A Reader's Guide*
	History of Canada: An Annotated Bibliography
Literature	*The Annotated Bibliography of Canada's Major Authors*
	MLA International Bibliography of Books and Articles on the Modern Languages and Literature
Music	*Music Reference and Research Materials*
	Bibliographic Guide to Music
Philosophy	*Oxford Companion to Philosophy*
	Research Guide to Philosophy
Religion	*Reference Works for Theological Research*
	Who's Who in Religion
Social Sciences	
Business	*Bibliographic Guide to Business and Economics*
	Business Information Sources
Education	*Education: A Guide to Reference and Information Sources*
	Resources in Education
Political Science	*International Bibliography of Political Science*
	Political Science: A Bibliographical Guide to the Literature
Psychology	*Psychology: A Guide to Reference and Information Sources*
	Bibliographical Guide to Psychology
Sociology	*Reference Sources in Social Work*
	Sociology: A Guide to Reference and Information Sources
Speech	*Research and Source Guide for Students in Speech Pathology and Audiology*
	Speech Monographs
Women's Studies	*Canadian Women in History*
	The Feminist Companion to Literature in English: Women Writers from the Middle Ages to the Present
	Readers' Guide to Women's Studies

Sciences

Astronomy	*The Cambridge Atlas of Astronomy*
	Dictionary of Astronomy
Biology	*Henderson's Dictionary of Biological Terms*
	Information Sources in the Life Sciences
Chemistry	*How to Find Chemical Information: A Guide for Practising*
	Chemists, Teachers, and Students
	Lange's Handbook of Chemistry
Computer	*ACM Guide to Computing Literature*
Science	*Bibliographic Guide to the History of Computing, Computers, and*
	the Information Processing Industry
Health	*Black's Medical Dictionary*
	Cumulated Index Medicus
Physics	*Information Sources in Physics*

2d Using Indexes to Find Magazine and Journal Articles

An index furnishes the exact page numbers to articles in magazines, journals, and newspapers. When you have a well-developed idea of your topic, go to the specialized indexes of your discipline, such as *Music Index* or *Philosopher's Index* (see the following lists). If labelled an *index*, it may or may not include an abstract. If labelled as an index to *abstracts,* each entry is an abstract. (*Note:* An abstract is a brief description of an article, usually written by the author.) An index to abstracts can accelerate your work by allowing you to read the abstract before you assume the task of locating and reading the entire work.

Starting with a General Index to Periodicals

On the library network, you have access to electronic databases such as *InfoTrac, Silverplatter, ProQuest, Academic Universe, EBSCOhost,* and others. One of these usually will guide you to several sources. For example, in response to the keyword search "child care and Canada" in *EBSCOhost,* a researcher would find more than 50 articles with abstracts. One example is shown in Figure 2.2.

The fight for a national child care system. (cover story)
CHILD care — Government policy
Canadian Dimension, Apr 92, Vol. 26 Issue 3, p15, 4p, 1 cartoon, 2bw
Ferguson, B.; Kassler, J.
> Discusses the struggle for high quality, universally accessible non-profit child care in Canada. Conference Board of Canada published research which identifies importance of employers addressing work and family life adjustment; Need for adequate child care contested by federal Tories; Child tax benefit; Funding; More

---

Figure 2.2
Source: EBSCOhost printout

If you click to retrieve more online data, you can read the full article.

For general information on current events, consult the *Readers' Guide to Periodical Literature,* which indexes such magazines as *Bioscience, Canadian Geographic, Foreign Affairs, Harvard Health Letter* and *Scientific Review.*

Searching Indexes to Topics in Specific Disciplines

2d

Consult the following indexes for articles in these specified disciplines:

Biology, zoology, botany, agriculture, and related fields: *Biological and Agricultural Index.*

Business, marketing, accounting, advertising, and related fields: *Business Periodicals Index.*

Canadian history, culture, and related fields: *Canadian Periodical Index.*

Chemistry, engineering, computer science, electronics, and related fields: *Applied Science and Technology Index.*

Education, physical education, and related fields: *Education Index.*

Film studies, theatre studies, and related fields: *International Index of Performing Arts.*

History, literature, philosophy, and related fields: *Humanities Index.*

Nursing and related fields: *Cumulative Index of Nursing and Allied Health (CINAHL).*

Sociology, psychology, and related fields: *Social Sciences Index.*

Searching an Index to Abstracts

Reading an index to abstracts (usually kept in the reference room) will accelerate your work. Only if the article appears promising will you need to read the entire article. Again, you can also use the electronic catalogue to find indexes such as these:

Abstracts of English Studies
Biological Abstracts
Chemical Abstracts
Humanities Abstracts
Psychological Abstracts
Sociological Abstracts

The following sample abstract from the journal *Essays on Canadian Writing,* Fall 2000, is in the *Humanities Abstracts* index.

Sandra Djwa, *"Here I Am": Atwood, Paper Houses, and a Parodic Tradition.*

The writer discusses the use of intertextual parody in Margaret Atwood's *Surfacing* and in other works of Canadian literature. *Surfacing* could be considered a prose anatomy of Canadian writing and culture up to the year of its publication. It incorporates allusions to a vast range of sources, from Northrop Frye to the entire tradition of the Canadian search for political identity and its literary articulation. Her parodic technique is respectful of the original texts she draws on, thus emphasizing the notion of continuity within discontinuity.

You may also wish to read the abstracts to the dissertations of graduate students, as listed in this reference source: *Dissertation Abstracts International.* Look for issue No. 12, Part II, of each volume, for it contains the cumulated subject and author indexes for issues 1–12 of the volume's two sections—*A: Humanities and Social Sciences* and *B: Sciences and Engineering.*

2e

Searching the Biographical Indexes for Authors and Personalities

When writing about a specific person, the reference section will provide multiple sources, some specific to a field, such as *American Men and Women of Science: The Physical and Biological Sciences* or *Who's Who in Hard Money Economics.* Several general indexes have value: *Biography Index: A Quarterly Index to Biographical Material in Books and Magazines, Current Biography Yearbook, Contemporary Authors,* and *Dictionary of Literary Biography.*

Searching Newspaper Indexes

Newspapers are a valuable resource because they provide contemporary information. Electronic networks enable you to find newspaper articles from across the world. Your library may have a newspaper search engine on its network, or you may need to go to the World Wide Web and access **Newspapers.com**. It will take you quickly to one of over 800 newspapers, from *The London Times* to *The Montreal Gazette.* In most cases, an online newspaper will have its own internal search engine that enables you to examine articles from its archives (see Chapter 3, page 28).

In addition, several print indexes, such as the following, are helpful, and are being placed online:

Globe and Mail: News and Services Index
New York Times Index
Official Index [to *The London Times*]

As well, most university and college libraries will have newspaper articles on microfilm (see "Using the Microforms," page 18).

2e Searching the Pamphlet Files and Pamphlet Indexes

Librarians collect bulletins, folders, pamphlets, and miscellaneous materials which they file alphabetically by subject in loose-leaf folders called the *pamphlet file* or *vertical file.* You should make the pamphlet file a regular stop during your preliminary investigation. It will have brochures on many topics, such as: "Asbestos in the Home," "Living with a Learning Disability," "Everything Doesn't Cause Cancer," and "Fetal Alcohol Syndrome."

For a preview of what the pamphlet files can contain, find one of these principal indexes to published pamphlets:

Vertical File Index: A Subject and Title Index to Selected Pamphlet Material. This work gives a description, the price, and information for ordering the pamphlet. Two helpful pamphlets, online and in print, are *SIRS* and *The CQ Researcher.*

Social Issues Resources Series (SIRS). This work collects articles on special topics and reprints them as one unit on a special subject—abortion, AIDS, prayer in schools, pollution. With *SIRS* you will have 10 or 12 articles readily available in one booklet.

The CQ Researcher, online and in print, will have pamphlets devoted to a single topic, such as "Energy and the Environment." Each pamphlet examines central issues on the topic, gives background information, shows a chronology of important events or processes, and provides an annotated bibliography. In one place you will have materials that can be quoted and paraphrased as well as a list of additional sources.

For the correct citation forms for articles found in *SIRS* or *The CQ Researcher,* see pages 99 and 100.

2f Searching for Government Documents

All branches of governments publish massive amounts of material, and many government documents have great value for researchers.

Useful print material includes the following:

Today on Parliament Hill. This daily newsletter is about the operation of the Parliament of Canada.

The Canada Gazette. This is the official newspaper of the Government of Canada since 1841.

For information about the government of the United States consult:

Public Affairs Information Service Bulletin. This work indexes articles and documents published by miscellaneous organizations.

The Congressional Record. This daily publication provides Senate and House legislative bills, documents, and reports.

Public Papers of the Presidents of the United States. This publication records the documents of the executive branch and the president, as well as members of the cabinet.

For useful online information on Canadian and International government publications see Chapter 3, page 24.

2g Searching for Essays within Books

The Essay and General Literature Index helps you find essays hidden within anthologies. It indexes material within books and collections of both a biographical and a critical nature. It enables you to find essays *within* books that you might otherwise overlook. The essay listed in the example below might easily have been overlooked by any researcher.

King, Martin Luther, 1929–1968

Raboteau, A. J. Martin Luther King, Jr. and the tradition of black religious protest (In *Religion and the life of the nation;* ed. by R. A. Sherrill, pp. 46–65.)

The electronic catalogue will give you the call number to Sherrill's book.

2h Using the Microforms

Libraries have a choice when ordering periodicals: they can buy expensive printed volumes or purchase moderately priced microform (microfilm or microfiche) versions of the same material. Most libraries have a mixture of the two. Most libraries now store national newspapers, weekly magazines, and dissertation abstracts on microfilm. Use a microfilm reader, usually located near the microfilm files, to browse the articles.

3   Searching the World Wide Web

L ike a library, the Internet serves as a major source of research information. It makes available millions of computer files relating to any subject—articles, illustrations, sound and video clips, and raw data. Entrance to this network is gained via the **World Wide Web (www),** a set of files accessed by means of a **browser,** such as *Netscape Navigator* or *Microsoft Explorer.* The connections between websites appear as **hypertext links**. Links are "hot" text or icons that, when clicked, instruct the computer to perform certain functions, such as to go to another file within this vast network (Web). You will know that text is hot when it is underlined and appears in a colour unlike the rest of the text.

The Internet cannot replace the library or field research. It offers the best and worst of information, so the material you find there requires careful evaluation. Before citing from an Internet article, take time to judge its authority and veracity. (See the checklist "Evaluating Internet Sources" in Chapter 3 on page 30.) This chapter will help you become an efficient searcher for academic information on the Internet.

3a   Using a Search Engine

When you know your topic, perform a keyword search by entering the words you would like to find in the title, description or text of an Internet source. The engine will direct you to a list of sites containing information about your topic. For example, to find information on the role of Tommy Douglas in the formation of Medicare you might enter *Tommy Douglas* and *Medicare* using a search engine like *Google.* The engine will direct you to a list of sites such as

> **www.savemedicare.com/y01ma00b.htm**
> **www.healthcoalition.ca/tommy.html**

You can then read the articles to determine if they relate to your research.

Using General Search Engines

Subject Directory Search Engines

These search engines are human compiled and hierarchical; they are indexed to guide you to general areas that are then subdivided into specific categories. Your choice of a category controls the search. You might start with *Canadian history,* move to *women's history,* move to *suffrage,* and arrive finally at

Nellie McClung. The sites found along the way may be useful and pertinent to your work. Examples of subject directory search engines are listed below:

About.com	**http:// about.com/aboutcanada**
Go.network	**www.go.com**
SympaticoLycos	**http://pre.sympatico.ca/index.jsp?lang=en_ca**
Yahoo!	**www.yahoo.ca**

Robot-Driven Search Engines

3a

These engines perform a keyword search by electronically scanning millions of web pages. Your key word phrase and Boolean operators (*and, or, not*) control the list. (See Tips for Keyword Searching below). For example, to find information on Pierre Trudeau's role in the October Crisis, you would enter the words *October Crisis* and *Pierre Trudeau.* The engine will direct you to a list of sites, such as: **www.clevernet.on.ca/pierre_trudeau/ links_pierre_trudeau.html** or **www.cbc.ca/millennium/timelines/ feature_octobercrisis.html**.

You can then read the articles to determine if they relate to your research efforts. Search engines usually put the most relevant sites first, so the first five or 10 will be likely sources. Here are examples of robot-driven search engines:

AltaVista Canada	**http://ca.altavista.com**
Excite	**www.excite.com**
Google Canada	**www.google.ca**
HotBot	**www.hotbot.com**
Webcrawler.ca	**www.webcrawler.ca**

Tips for Keyword Searching

1. If you write a single word (e.g., *trudeau*), you often will get a mammoth list of sites containing the term, most having little relevance to your topic. Generally, it is better to search with more than one word.
   Note: Lower case words will find capitalized words (e.g., *trudeau* will find *trudeau, Trudeau,* and *TRUDEAU*).

2. If you provide two or more words with *and* between each one, the search engine will find only sources that combine all words: trudeau *and* October Crisis *and* War Measures Act.

3. Attach a + in front of words that *must* appear in documents and a – in front of words that *must not* appear: *trudeau + October Crisis – Robert Bourassa.* This request will give you documents that mention *trudeau* and the *October Crisis* but will eliminate any documents that include Bourassa's name.

4. You may also use *not* to eliminate a term: Margaret Atwood *and* poetry *not* fiction. This request will focus the search on sites about Margaret Atwood and her poetry but not her fiction.

5. Use a *t:* to restrict the search to a title: *t: war measures act.*

6. Use quotation marks around two words to make them one unit (although proper names do not need quotation marks): "stonehenge + Thomas Hardy". This request will give you documents that combine both Stonehenge and Thomas Hardy. The use of phrases is perhaps the best way to limit the number of hits by the search engine. Compare:

October Crisis and 1970 (150 000 documents found)
"The October Crisis of 1970" (306 documents found)

Therefore, make your request with phrases inside quotation marks without the *and* whenever possible; that is, ask for "migraine headaches" (2000 hits), not "migraine and headaches" (10 000 hits).

. 3b

Metasearch Engines

A metasearch engine simultaneously queries about 10 major search engines, such as those listed above, and provides you with a short, relevant set of results. You get fewer results than would appear at one of the major search engines. For example, "chocolate + children" produced 342 718 results on *AltaVista* but only 50 on *Mamma.com*. A metasearch engine selects the first few listings from each of the search engines under the theory that each engine puts the most relevant results at the top of its list. Here are three metasearch engines:

Dogpile.com	**www.dogpile.com**
Mamma.com	**http://mamma.com**
Metacrawler.com	**www.metacrawler.com/index.htm**

3b Using Search Engines Devoted to Academic Disciplines

Many search engines specialize in one area, such as *ERIC* (Education) or *Envirolink* (Environmental Studies). The following list contains sites that may be helpful in launching your investigation of Internet resources.

Humanities

Voice of the Shuttle **http://vos.ucsb.edu** provides a massive collection of bibliographies, textual criticism, news groups, and links to numerous fields in the humanities.

> **Hint:** If you have problems accessing a particular website, try truncating the address: that is, cut items from the end. For example, cut **www.nlc-bnc.ca/caninfo/ ecaninfo.htm** to **www.nlc-bnc.ca**. At the main page of this site, you can search for whatever file you need.

Art

Canadian Artists on the Web (CAW) **www.CanadianArtistsOnTheWeb.ca** provides information on living Canadian painters, sculptors, digital artists, printmakers, photographers and installation artists who offer collections of images of their work on the Web.

WebMuseum, Paris **www.ibiblio.org/wm** gives information on ancient and classical art, the Renaissance, 19th-century American works, impressionism, and many other periods. It also links you to major museums and their collections.

World Wide Arts Resources **http://wwar.world-arts-resources.com** provides an index of artists, exhibits, festivals, meetings, and performances. Its search engine takes you to fine arts departments, online courses, syllabi, and art institutions.

Canadian Studies

Canadian Information by Subject **www.nlc-bnc.ca/caninfo/ecaninfo. htm** supplies a great deal of information about Canada from Internet resources around the world.

National Library of Canada Collections **www.nlc-bnc.ca/6** provides links to works in all subjects written by, about, or of interest to Canadians, published in Canada or abroad.

History

Canadian History Time Line **http://web.securenet.net/members/ chastie/Hisintro.html** gives a great deal of historical information conveniently categorized chronologically, as well as many useful links to resources on Canadian history, politics and culture.

Humbul Humanities Hub **http://humbul.ac.uk** from the University of Oxford provides historical resources, references, libraries, and bulletin boards, with links to downloadable texts, as well as links to resources in other fields in the humanities.

Literature

Canadian Literature **www.canlit.ca/resources** provides valuable links to websites on archival Canadian literature, Canadian journals and literary magazines, Canadian children's literature, Canadian poetry and a host of other Canadian Literature resources.

English Server eserver **http://eserver.org** provides academic resources in the humanities, including drama, fiction, film, television, and history, including full text documents, plus a link for downloading freeware and shareware.

Literature Directory **http://dmoz.org/Arts/Literature** provides a wide-ranging directory, with links, to a vast amount of information on American, British, Canadian, and World literature, including links to many scholarly journals.

Northwest Passages Canadian Literature online **www.nwpassages.com/ canlitlinks.asp** provides an enormous amount of information on

3b

general Canadian literature, Canadian studies programs and associations, Canadian authors and publishers, and Canadian literary periodicals and literary organizations.

Philosophy

Philosophy Web Sites **www.uh.edu/~cfreelan/SWIP/philos.html** provides a list of links to websites such as *A Guide to Philosophy on the Internet* and *HIPPIAS,* a peer-reviewed search engine for philosophy.

Religion

Canadian Society for the Study of Religion (CSSR/SCSR) **www.ccsr.ca/ cssr/Acadlink.html** provides links to resources and research in religious studies (not confined to Canadian sources).

Comparative Religion **http://weber.u.washington.edu/~madin** gives references and resources for all religions and religious studies and religious organizations.

Business

All Business Network **www.all-biz.com** provides a search engine to businesses, with relevant information for newsletters, organizations, newsgroups, and magazines.

Nijenrode Business Webserver **http://library.nijenrode.nl/INT/index. html** serves primarily students and faculty at business schools, with a search engine that finds news, business journals, career opportunities in accounting, banking, finance, marketing, and related fields.

Communication

Communication Resources on the Web **http://alnilam.ucs.indiana. edu:1027/sources/networks.html** takes you to resources and websites on associations, book reviews, bibliographies, libraries, media, information science programs, and departments of communication in various universities.

Education

Canadian Education on the Web **www.oise.utoronto.ca/~mpress/ eduweb/eduweb.html**, developed by the Ontario Institute for Studies in Education (OISE), has links to all aspects of Canadian education, including academic resources, associations and organizations, educators, elementary, secondary, and post-secondary programs, and more.

Educational Resource and Information Center (ERIC) **http://ericir. syr.edu/ithome**, the primary source of research information for most educators, contains about one million documents, available by a keyword search, on all aspects of teaching and learning, lesson plans, administration, bibliographies, and a wide array of classroom-related topics.

Government

Canadian Government Information on the Internet (CGII) **http://cgii.gc.ca/index-e.html**, with a link to the Government of Canada Primary Internet Site, supplies information on the Government of Canada, its programs and services.

Oultwood **www.oultwood.com/localgov/canada.htm** gives information on provincial and local government in Canada, as well as many links to other provincial resources.

HR-NET **www.hri.org/nodes/intl.html#gen** provides a vast number of links to websites on the government, culture and history of over 200 countries, as well as valuable information on international affairs.

Political Science

Canadian Politics on the Web **http://polisci.nelson.com/canpol.html** provides annotated links to hundreds of websites dealing with Canadian politics and government, with many connections to full-text documents.

Political Science Resources on the Web **www.lib.umich.edu/govdocs/polisci.html** is a vast data file on government information at all levels, domestic and international. It is a useful site for political theory and international relations, with links to dissertations, periodicals, reference sources, university courses, and other social science information.

Psychology

Educational Psychology Resources Online **www.library.ualberta.ca/subject/edpsych/websites** from the University of Alberta provides resources in educational psychology, special education, counselling and school psychology, with links to American, Canadian and International Psychological associations and publications.

Psych Web **www.psychwww.com** features articles from *Psychiatric Times*, reports from the National Institutes of Health, information from universities, and links to psychology journals and other websites. It includes Freud's *The Interpretation of Dreams*.

Sociology

Recommended Web Sites in Sociology **www.library.ualberta.ca/subject/sociology/websites/index.cfm** from the University of Alberta is a very helpful site listing websites supplying information on Canadian social policy, sociological theory and theorists, and other related topics.

Sociology Praxis **http://wizard.ucr.edu/praxis.discuss.html** provides a massive collection of articles on socioeconomic topics, with links to other social science resources.

Sociology **http://hakatai.mcli.dist.maricopa.edu/smc/ml/sociology.html** gives access to hundreds of websites that provide articles and resource materials on almost all aspects of sociology issues.

3b

Women's Studies

Web Sites for Women's Studies **www.library.ubc.ca/wmst/web.html** from the University of British Columbia provides a comprehensive list of Asian, Canadian, European and U.S. websites for women's studies, as well as links to e-journals and more.

Women's Studies Resources **www.lib.umd.edu/UMCP/ETC/SUBR/ resources.women_studies.html** features a search engine for a keyword search to women's issues and provides directories to bibliographies, classic texts, references, course syllabi from various universities, and links to other websites.

Astronomy

Canadian Astronomical Websites **www.seameadow.com/canast.html** provides over 100 links to Canadian institutes and departments of astronomy, the Canadian National and Regional Astronomical Societies, planetariums and the space industry in Canada.

American Astronomical Society **www.aas.org** supplies the *Astrophysical Journal*, providing articles, reviews, and educational information. It gives links to other astronomical websites.

Northern Lights Planetarium, Norway **www.uit.no/npt/homepage-npt. en.html** takes you into the planetarium, displays the northern lights in vivid colours, and enables you to research such topics as *Aurora Borealis*.

Computer and Internet Technology

canadacomputes.com **www.canadacomputes.com** provides Canadian focused computer product reviews, industry news, tutorials, publications and interviews with leading Canadian technology figures.

Internet Society **www.isoc.org** is supported by the companies, agencies, and foundations that launched the Internet and keep it functioning. It gives you vital information, with articles from the ISOC Forum newsletter.

Byte Magazine **www.byte.com** brings you a wealth of full-text articles, online magazines, technical documents, and links to high-tech issues.

Environmental Science

Envirolink **http://envirolink.org** has a search engine that allows access to environmental articles, photographs, action alerts, organizations, and additional Web sources.

Environmental Association of Canada (ESAC) **www.thegreenpages.ca/ esac/index.htm** provides links to Canadian environmental organizations, environmental studies programs, and academic resources relevant to the environmental community.

General Science

Academy of Natural Sciences Related Links **www.acnatsci.org/ links.html** supplies links to hundreds of articles and resource materials on various issues and topics in the natural sciences.

National Academy of Sciences **www.nas.edu** combines the resources of the National Academy of Engineering, the Institute of Medicine, and the National Research Council. It focuses on math and science education and has links to scientific societies.

Health and Medicine

Global Health Network **www.pitt.edu/HOME/GHNet.html** supplies access to documents in public health provided by scholars at the World Health Organization, NASA, Pan American Health Organization, and others. It has links to agencies, organizations, and health networks.

Health Canada Online **www.hc-sc.gc.ca** provides information on topics from cancer and diabetes to malpractice and medical ethics. It supplies links to online journals and magazines for the most recent news in medical science.

> ***Hint:*** You can quickly build a bibliography on the Internet in two ways: (1) at a search engine on the Internet, such as *AltaVista,* enter a descriptive phrase, such as "Child Abuse Bibliographies," and (2) use the search engines of **Amazon.com** and **chapters.indigo.ca** to gain a list of books currently in print. In most cases, the books on these lists will be available in your library.

3c Accessing Online Sources

Several types of online sources are available; try more than one type in your research.

Locating Home Pages

You can locate home pages for individuals, institutions, and organizations by using a search engine, such as *Yahoo!* or *AltaVista.* Type in a person's name or the name of an organization, such as the American Psychological Association, and you will get a link to the site, such as **www.apa.org**. The home page will provide links, a directory, an index, or an internal search engine that will take you quickly to specific material.

Accessing Web Articles

A search engine will direct you to many articles on the Internet, some isolated without documentation and credentials and others that list the author as well as the association to which the author belongs. For example, a search for "child care centres" will produce local websites, such as "Apple Tree Family Child Care." Private websites like these will infuse your research with local knowledge. Adding another relevant term such as "child care regulations" will take you to provincial and national websites, such as "Child & Family Canada."

Finding Journal Articles

The Internet supplies journal articles of two types. Some appear in original online journals designed and published only on the Web. Others are reproductions of articles that have appeared in printed journals. In either case, you can find journal articles in several ways.

- Using your favourite search engine, enter a keyword phrase for *journals* plus the name of your subject. For example, one student using *Google* entered "journals + aboriginal" and found links to numerous journals, such as *Ayaangwaamizin: International Journal of Indigenous Philosophy,* and *The Canadian Journal of Native Studies.*
- Access a search engine's subject directory. In *Yahoo!,* for example, one student selected "Social Science" from the directory, clicked on Sociology, clicked on Journals, and accessed links to several online journals, such as *Sociological Research Online* and *Edge: The E-Journal of Intercultural Relations.*
- Access an electronic database like *EBSCOhost* **www.ebscohost.com** and select "Academic Search Elite." A keyword search will direct you to the full text of over 1500 journal articles in the social sciences, humanities, general science, and many other disciplines.
- If you already know the name of a journal, go to your favourite search engine to make a keyword query, such as *Canadian Journal of Philosophy.*

Note: Some journals require a fee or require you to join the association before they permit access to you.

Hint: Remember that abstracts may not accurately represent the full article. In fact, some abstracts are not written by the author at all but by an editorial staff. Resist the desire to quote from the abstract; instead, write a paraphrase or, better, find the full text and cite from it.

Finding Magazine Articles

Some magazine articles appear in original online magazines designed and published only on the Web. Others are reproductions of articles that have appeared in printed magazines. Several directories exist for searching magazine articles.

Canadian Magazine Publishers Association (CMPA) **www.cmpa.ca** provides a list of Canadian magazines, relevant tables of contents and article titles. Full text is not available.

EBSCOhost **www.ebscohost.com** provides full text for nearly 190 popular Canadian and American general interest, health and science magazines. Click on the database Canadian MAS FullTEXT Elite.

NewsDirectory.com **www.newsdirectory.com/new** takes you to magazine home pages where you can begin your search in a magazine's archives. Under "current events," for example, you can access *Newsweek* **Newsweek.com** or *Maclean's* **Macleans.ca**.

3c

Pathfinder **www.time.com/time/index.htm** gives free access to *Time Magazine* and has a good search engine to thousands of archival articles.

ZD Net **www.zdnet.com** provides excellent access to industry-oriented articles in banking, electronics, computers, and management. It offers two weeks of free access before charges begin to accrue.

3c

You can also access online magazine articles through the directory of a search engine such as *AltaVista* or *Google*. (See "Finding Journal Articles" on page 27.)

Accessing News Sources

Most major news organizations maintain Internet sites. A simple way of accessing these sites is through the search engine *Google*. Click on "News and Resources" in the directory on the *Google* home page and you will have access to over 70 national and international news organizations, such as the following:

Canadian News Sources

CBC.ca	**www.cbc.ca**
The Globe and Mail	**www.theglobeandmail.com**
National Post Online	**www.nationalpost.com**

U.S. News Sources

CNN.com	**www.cnn.com**
New York Times on the Web	**www.nytimes.com**
USA Today	**www.usatoday.com**

International News Sources

BBC News (Great Britain)	**http://news.bbc.co.uk**
International Herald Tribune	**www.iht.com**
The Times of India	**http://timesofindia.indiatimes.com**

To find additional newspapers, search for "newspapers" on *AltaVista, Google,* or *Yahoo!* Your college or university library may also provide *LEXIS-NEXIS*, which will search online news sources for you.

> **Hint:** In your documentation, refer to the Internet source to avoid giving the appearance that you are citing from the printed version. There are sometimes major differences between the same article in, for example, *The National Post* and in *National Post Online*.

Note: After you find the journal, magazine, or newspaper of your choice, make a bookmark so you can access it quickly.

Accessing Books on the Web

One of the best sources of full-text, online books is the Online Books Page at the University of Pennsylvania: **http://digital.library.upenn.edu/books**. This site indexes books by author, title, and subject. Its search engine quickly takes you to the full text of William Wordsworth's *Lyrical Ballads*, or to Elizabeth Tucker's *Leaves from Juliana Horatia Ewing's "Canada Home."* This site is adding new textual material almost every day, so consult it first. Understand, however, that contemporary books, still under copyright protection, are not included. That is, you can freely download an Oscar Wilde novel but not one by Margaret Atwood.

Here are a few additional sites:

Bartleby.com	**www.bartleby.com**
Early Canadiana Online	**www.canadiana.org**
Internet Classics Archive	**http://classics.mit.edu**
Project Gutenberg	**http://promo.net/pg**
Bibliomania	**www.bibliomania.com**
Online Literary Criticism Collection	**www.ipl.org/ref/litcrit**
Victorian Women Writers' Project	**www.indiana.edu/~letrs/vwwp**

There are many more; some sites, such as Bibliomania, provide selected study guides and reference resources as well as free texts. In a search engine, use a keyword request for "full-text books."

3d Using Listserv, Usenet, and Other Protocols

Communication on the Internet can be asynchronous, in which you post and receive messages at different times as in e-mail, or synchronous, in which you communicate simultaneously with others in a chat room.

Participating in Listserv

The word *listserv* describes discussion groups that correspond via e-mail about a specific educational or technical subject. For example, your literature professor might ask everybody in the class to join a listserv group on Victorian literature. To participate, you must have an e-mail address and subscribe to the list.

To access a national listserv, consult one of these sites:

L-Soft **www.lsoft.com/products/default.asp?itemilistserv** catalogues the more than 42 000 public listserv lists on the Internet.

Egroups **www.groups.yahoo.com** allows you to join a listserv group in such areas as health and fitness, home, recreation, reference and education, science, sports, and others.

Topica **www.topica.com** allows you to search thousands of newsletters and discussions on topics such as personal technology, health and fitness, and art and design.

Tile.Net **www.tile.net** provides access to lists, usenet news groups, and FTP sites.

Each site will explain the procedure for subscribing and participating via e-mail in a discussion.

Participating in Chat Rooms and Open Forums

Usenet and chat groups use Internet sites where all users can participate at once. To access one of the open forums on a usenet network, go to **dogpile.com** or **metacrawler.com** and click the *usenet* button before launching the search. Typing "diabetes" would take you to a site such as **alt.support.diabetes** for such topics as "Is diabetes increasing?" or "Symptoms of diabetes." These discussions, in the main, are serious commentaries by persons with a personal stake in the subject. If the site includes the real name of the person speaking, along with an e-mail address, they might be used in a research paper, but you have no way of authenticating the person's credentials. Thus, let the reader know something about the source: "Lori Silfen in a recent usenet conversation reminded her audience to refer to 'a person with diabetes,' not to a 'diabetic person.'"

3d

Evaluating Internet Sources

Here are a few guidelines to help you make judgments about the validity and veracity of Internet sources.

- Prefer the "edu" and "org" sites. Usually these are domains developed by an educational institution, such as Ohio State University, or by a professional organization, such as the American Psychological Association. However, "edu" sites also include student papers that can include unreliable information.

- The "gov" (government) and "mil" (military) sites usually have reliable materials. The "com" (commercial) sites become suspect for several reasons: (1) they are selling advertising space, (2) they often charge you for access to their files, and (3) they can be ISP (Internet Service Provider) sites that people pay to use and to post material. Although some ISP sites have good information, they are usually quite unreliable.

- Look for the professional affiliation of the writer, which you will find in the opening credits or an e-mail address. Go in search of the writer's home page. Type in the writer's name at a search engine to see how many results are listed. Type in the writer's name at **Amazon.com** for a list of his or her books. If you find no information on the writer, you should probably abandon the source and look elsewhere.

- Look for a bibliography that accompanies the article, which will indicate the scholarly nature of this writer's work.

- Usenet discussion groups offer valuable information at times, but some articles lack sound, fundamental reasoning or evidence to support the opinions.

- Treat e-mail and chat messages as mail, not as scholarly articles.

- Does the site give you hypertext links to professional sites or to commercial sites? Links to educational sites serve as a bibliography to more reliable sources. Links to commercial sites are often attempts to sell you something.

- Learn to distinguish among the different types of websites, such as advocacy pages, personal home pages, informational pages, and business and marketing pages. One site provides evaluation techniques; see **www.science.widener.edu/~withers/webeval.htm**.

4   Collecting Data Outside the Library

The library and the World Wide Web certainly contain invaluable sources, but information can sometimes be found in other places. Conduct primary research in the laboratory and in the field whenever your topic permits it. Investigate local sources, examine audiovisual materials, and conduct a survey if the results will be relevant to your research.

4a Investigating Local Sources

Interviewing Knowledgeable People

Personal interviews with knowledgeable people can elicit valuable in-depth information about your subject. Look for experienced persons at organizations such as the provincial or municipal historian's office, a senior citizens' organization, or a local historical society. Another way to accomplish this task is to request information on a listserv list, which will bring you commentary from experts interested in a particular field. (See Chapter 3, page 29, "Using Listserv, Usenet, and Other Protocols," for more details.)

Prepare several pertinent, focused questions. For accuracy, use a tape recorder (with the permission of the person interviewed). Conduct telephone interviews only if you find them necessary. Consult with several people, if possible, and weigh their different opinions.

Keep in mind three criteria for the interview:

- Consult with experienced persons.
- Be courteous and on time for interviews.
- Be prepared with a set of questions for initiating the interview.

Writing Letters and Corresponding by E-mail

Correspondence, whether by letter or e-mail, provides a written record for research. Ask pointed questions so that correspondents will respond directly to your central issues.

Dear Ms. Carriere:

I am a university student conducting research on gender language differences in emotional expression. Since you have expertise in this area, I would appreciate your assistance. In particular, I need specific information on the main differences in the content of male and female conversations.

> May I quote you in my report? I will honour your request to withhold your name. I have enclosed a stamped, self-addressed envelope for your convenience, or you may e-mail me at gsmythe@umanitoba.ca.
>
> Sincerely,
>
>
> Glayne Smythe

This letter makes a fairly specific request for information. If Glayne Smythe uses a quotation from the reply, she should provide a bibliography entry in her Works Cited page.

> Carriere, A. Advisor, Access Programme, University of Manitoba, Winnipeg, MB. E-mail to the author. 5 Apr 2002.

Remember to sign your name as well as to type it, and as a courtesy, do not forget to write a thank-you note when you receive a reply. If the correspondence is by e-mail, you can thank your correspondent immediately.

Reading Personal Papers

Search out letters, diaries, manuscripts, family histories, and other personal materials that might contribute to your study. The city library may house private collections, and the city librarian can usually help you contact the county historian and other private citizens who have important documents. Obviously, handling private papers must be done with the utmost decorum and care. Make a bibliography entry for such materials:

> Houston, James. "Notes on the Fiddlers of Cape Breton Island." Unpublished paper. Ingonish, 1995.

Attending Lectures and Public Addresses

Watch bulletin boards and the newspaper for a featured speaker who might visit your campus. Take careful notes and, if necessary, request a copy of the lecture or speech. Remember, too, that many lectures, reproduced on video, will be available in the library or in departmental files.

Investigating Government Documents

Documents are available at three levels of government—municipal, provincial, and federal. As a constituent, you are entitled to the services of various agencies. If your topic demands it, contact the mayor's office, attend a city council meeting, or search out printed documents or online information.

Municipal Government

Visit the appropriate municipal or city office to find facts on elections, censuses, marriages, births, and deaths. The archives may include information on wills, taxes, property deeds, zoning plans, traffic projections, flood control, and other official documents.

Provincial Government

Contact by phone a provincial government office that relates to your research, such as Aboriginal Affairs, Consumer and Corporate Affairs, Department of Health, or Education and Training. The agencies may vary by name in your province or territory. Remember, too, that the province or territory will have an archival storehouse for its records, which are also available for public review.

Federal Government

A Canadian senator or Member of Parliament can send booklets printed by federal departments and agencies. For more information see the Depository Services Program (DPS) website **http://dsp-psd.communication.gc.ca/ search_form-e.html**. In addition, you can go to the National Archives Building in Ottawa, or to one of the regional branches in the provinces and territories. These archives contain government documents which you can review. Also, consult the National Archives of Canada website at **www. archives.ca**.

4d

4b Examining Audiovisual Materials, Television, and Radio

Important data can be found in audiovisual materials: films, filmstrips, music, phonograph recordings, slides, audio cassettes, compact disc recordings, video cassettes, and DVDs. You will find these sources both on and off campus. Consult such guides as *Educators' Guide* (film, filmstrips, and tapes), *Media Review Digest* (non-print materials), *Video Source Book* (video catalogue), *The Film File,* or *International Index to Recorded Poetry.*

Numerous television programs of quality are available if you watch the schedules carefully. In particular, check the programming of the Public Broadcasting System, Discovery Channel, History Channel, and Arts and Entertainment. In addition, national and local talk shows often discuss important issues. Remember to keep accurate notes on names, statements, program titles, and production dates.

4c Conducting a Survey with a Questionnaire

Questionnaires can produce original, first-hand data that you can tabulate and analyze. The information will be current, localized, and suited to your research. Of course, to achieve meaningful results, you must survey a random sample, one that is large enough and representative of the whole population in terms of age, sex, race, education, income, residence, and other factors. Various degrees of bias can creep into the questionnaire unless you remain objective. Thus, use the formal survey as an information-obtaining device when you are experienced with tests and measurements as well as with statistical analysis, or when you have an instructor who will help you with the survey.

4d Writing a Case Study

A case study is a formal report based upon your observation of a human subject. For example, you might examine patterns of behaviour to build a profile of a person based on biographical data, interviews, tests, and observation. The case study then becomes evidence for your research paper. Each discipline has its own ways of conducting a case study, and you should not begin examining any subject without the guidance of your instructor or supervisor. In fact, certain laws govern your work with human subjects.

4e Conducting Experiments, Tests, and Measurements

Empirical research, often performed in a laboratory or within a controlled setting, is another source of original data. It determines why and how things exist, function, or interact with one another. Again, each discipline has its own conventions, both for conducting an experiment and for writing about it. Generally, your paper will explain your methods and findings in pursuit of a hypothesis (your thesis). An experiment thereby becomes primary evidence for your paper.

For example, your experiments with bull trout populations at a test site near Great Bear Lake would require you to write a report that would provide four distinct parts:

Introduction to state the hypothesis and how it relates to the problem, to provide the theoretical implications of the study, and to explain the manner in which this study relates to previously published work.

Method to describe what you did and how you conducted the study: the subjects who participated, whether human or animal; your equipment and how you used it; and the procedure at each stage of your work.

Results to report your findings and to provide the necessary statistical treatment of the findings by means of tables, graphs, and charts.

Discussion to explain the implications of your work, to interpret the findings, and to discuss the implications of the findings.

Your experiment and the writing of the report will require the attention of your instructors. Seek their advice often.

At this point in your research, you should have a working bibliography of sources from books, from printed articles in journals and/or magazines, from the Internet, and, if appropriate, from notes and data of planned research through interviews, observation, and experiments. Now you are ready to organize your ideas and set goals for writing your paper.

5 Organizing Ideas and Setting Goals

During the search for source materials, you should organize your ideas so that reading and note taking will relate directly to your specific needs. Your notes must grow from carefully drawn plans, which may include a research proposal, a list of ideas or questions, or a rough outline. In addition, the design of your study might match an appropriate academic model, called a *paradigm* (see 5b, pages 37–40). This chapter includes instructions for crafting a formal outline, which may need to accompany your final manuscript.

5a Charting a Direction and Setting Goals

Do not plunge too quickly into note taking. You need to know *what* to look for and *why* you need it; therefore, frame your key ideas in a chart or outline. Thereby, you will have the necessary terminology for labelling your notes. The following activities will assist you in the writing process.

Writing a Research Proposal

Your **research proposal** (see pages 7–8) introduces issues that you will need to investigate. For example, the last sentence of the following research proposal names four topics worthy of research.

> I want to address young people who think they need a tan to be beautiful. Preliminary investigation indicates that ultraviolet radiation causes severe skin damage that is cumulative; that is, radiation builds adverse effects with each exposure. My role is to investigate the facts and explore options for those who desire a good tan. I need information on skin types, sun exposure, tanning beds, and types of skin damage.

Listing Key Words and Phrases

Listing key words and phrases focuses your research using the terms most important to your issue. Jot down ideas or words in a rough list and then expand the list to show a hierarchy of major and minor ideas. One researcher started with this set of key words:

natural sun	tanning beds
sunscreens	time in the sun
skin damage	ultraviolet radiation

The researcher could use these words as the tag lines to begin each note.

Developing a Rough Outline

A rough outline will arrange the words and phrases to show the hierarchy of the issues.

> The tanning process
>> Natural sun
>> Artificial light at tanning salons
>> Time in the sun or under the screen
>
> Effects of radiation on the skin
>> Immediate skin damage
>> Long-term skin damage
>
> Protection
>> Oils
>> Sunscreens
>> Time control

5a

This outline, although sketchy, provides the terminology for scanning sources, checking alphabetical indexes, and conducting interviews or questionnaires (see 4a and 4c, pages 31 and 33).

Generating a List of Questions about Your Topic

A list of questions about your topic will invite you to develop answers on note cards.

> Is there such a thing as a healthy tan?
> How does a tan differ from "sunburn"?
> What causes skin damage?
> How prevalent is skin damage?
> What are the short-term consequences of sunburn?
> What are the long-term consequences of sunburn?

You should try to answer every question with at least one note, as shown here:

> Skin damage   Rennick 63
>
> No tan is healthy. "Anything that damages the skin—and burning certainly does that—cannot be considered safe" (Rennick 63).

Using Modes of Development

Modes of development can help you build effective paragraphs. One writer developed this list:

> <u>Define</u> sunburn
>
> <u>Contrast</u> natural tanning with tanning bed tans
>
> <u>Illustrate</u> sunburn with several examples
>
> Use <u>statistics</u> and <u>scientific data</u>
>
> Search out <u>causes</u> with a focus on the sun and its ultraviolet rays
>
> Determine the <u>consequences</u> of burning
>
> Use a <u>case study</u>

Explore the step-by-step stages of the <u>process</u>

<u>Classify</u> the types and <u>analyze</u> the problem

Give <u>narrative</u> examples

With this list in hand, the writer can search for material to develop a paper as *contrast, process, definition,* and so forth.

Approaching Your Topic in Different Ways

Different academic disciplines, each with a special insight into any given area, will approach the same topic in different ways. Suppose, for example, that you wish to examine an event from Canadian history, such as the October Crisis of 1970. Four different approaches might be as follows:

POLITICAL SCIENCE	The political ambitions of Pierre Trudeau may have propelled him into hasty action during the October Crisis of 1970.
ENGLISH	In his novel *Prochain Épisode*, Hubert Aquin argues passionately for the type of violent revolution witnessed in the October Crisis of 1970.
ECONOMICS	The October Crisis of 1970 was the inevitable outcome of the abject poverty suffered by some French Canadians during the 1960s.
SOCIOLOGY	An example of an ethnic group's need to establish its separate identity is the Quiet Revolution which culminated in the October Crisis of 1970.

5b

5b Using Academic Models (Paradigms) to Stimulate Your Note Taking

A *paradigm* is a plan that governs most papers of a given type. It is not content specific; rather, it provides an organizational model and a basic pattern for many different papers. In contrast, an outline is a specific plan for one paper only; so, start with a paradigm and finish with an outline.

A General All-Purpose Model

If you have any hesitation about the design of your paper, start with this bare-bones model and expand it with your material. Readers, including your instructor, are accustomed to this sequence for research papers. It offers plenty of leeway.

Identify the subject
    Explain the problem
    Provide background information
    Frame a thesis statement
Analyze the subject
    Examine the first major issue
    Examine the second major issue
    Examine the third major issue

Discuss your findings
Restate your thesis and point beyond it
Interpret the findings
Provide answers, solutions, a final judgment

To the introduction you can add a quotation, an anecdote, a definition, and other material. Within the body you can compare, analyze, give evidence, trace historical events, and handle many other matters. In the conclusion you can challenge an assumption, take exception to a prevailing point of view, and reaffirm your thesis. All of these devices are discussed in detail in 8e, pp. 79–83.

A Model for Advancing Your Ideas and Theories

If you want to advance a theory in your paper, adjust this next design to fit your needs. Eliminate some items and add new elements as necessary.

Introduction
Establish the problem or question
Discuss its significance
Provide necessary background information
Introduce experts who have addressed the problem
Provide a thesis statement that addresses the problem from a
perspective not yet advanced by others
Body
Trace issues involved in the problem
Develop a past-to-present examination
Compare and analyze the details and minor issues
Cite experts who have addressed the same problem
Conclusion
Advance and defend your theory as it grows out of evidence in
the body
Offer directives or a plan of action
Suggest additional work and research that is needed

A Model for the Analysis of Creative Works

If you plan a literary analysis of poetry, fiction, or drama or if you must study music, art, or other artistic works, adjust this next paradigm to your subject and purposes:

Introduction
Identification of the work (brief summary in one sentence)
Background information that relates to the author
Biographical facts about the author that relate to the specific issues
Quotations and paraphrases of authorities that establish the scholarly
traditions
Thesis statement that establishes your particular views of the literary
work or other art form

Body
> An analysis divided according to such elements as imagery, theme, character development, structure, symbolism, narration, language, and so forth

Conclusion
> A focus on the work's author, not just on the analysis in the essay's body
>
> In particular, a conclusion that explores the contributions of the writer in concord with your thesis sentence

A Model for Argument or Persuasion Papers

If you must write persuasively or argue from a set position, your paper should conform in general to this next paradigm. Select the elements that fit your design.

Introduction
> A statement that establishes the problem or controversial issue that your paper will examine
>
> A summary of the issues
>
> Definition of key terminology
>
> A concession on some points of the argument
>
> Quotation and paraphrase of sources to build the controversial nature of the subject
>
> Background information to establish past theories and current ideas on the topic
>
> A thesis statement to establish your position

Body
> Arguments in defence of one side
>
> Analysis of the issues, both pro and con
>
> Evidence from the sources, including quotations

Conclusion
> Your thesis expanded into a conclusion that makes clear your position, which should be one that grows logically from your analysis and discussion of the issues

5b

A Model for a Comparative Study

Writing a comparative study will require you to examine two schools of thought, two issues, or the positions taken by two persons. The paper compares and contrasts the issues, as outlined in the following general plan that offers three arrangements for the body of the paper.

Introduction
> Introduction of A
>
> Introduction of B
>
> Brief comparison of the two
>
> Introduction of the central issues
>
> Citation of source materials on the subjects
>
> Presentation of your thesis statement

Body (choose one)

Examine A	Similarities of A & B	Issue 1
		Discuss A & B
Examine B	Differences of A & B	Issue 2
		Discuss A & B
Compare &	Discussion of central	Issue 3
contrast A & B	issues	Discuss A & B

Conclusion

Discussion of significant issues
Conclusion that ranks one over the other
or
Conclusion that rates the respective merit of each side

Remember that the formulas provided above are general guidelines, not iron-clad rules. Adjust each as necessary to meet your special needs.

5c Using Your Thesis to Direct Your Research

After you have identified the paradigm appropriate to your assignment, you will have a better feel for writing your thesis statement. Your thesis will set the tone and direction of your paper. Below your thesis sentence, **list concepts** that will expand upon the thesis, as shown next:

THESIS Television can have positive effects on a child's language development.

1. Television introduces new words.
2. Television reinforces word usage and proper syntax.
3. Literary classics come alive verbally on TV.
4. Television provides the subtle rhythms and musical effects of the best speakers.

The outline above gives the writer four categories that require detailed research in support of the thesis. For help in refining your thesis statement, see 8b, pages 71–73.

5d Writing a Formal Outline

A formal outline classifies the issues of your study into clear, logical categories with main headings and one or more subheadings. Not all papers require a formal outline, nor do some researchers need one. A short research paper can be created from key words, a list of issues, a rough outline, and a rough draft.

However, many writers benefit by developing a formal outline that classifies the investigation into clear, logical divisions. The outline will give unity and coherence to your miscellaneous handwritten notes, computer drafts, and photocopied materials. It helps to change miscellaneous notes into an ordered progression of ideas.

Note: A formal outline is not rigid and inflexible; you may, and should, modify it while writing and revising.

> ***Hint:*** You may wish to experiment with the Outline feature of your word processor. If you use the feature when composing the original document, it will allow you to view the paper at various levels of detail and to "drag and drop" the essay into a different organization.

Using Standard Outline Symbols

List your major categories and subtopics in this form:

I. First major heading
   A. _____ Subheading of first degree
       1. _____ Subheadings of second degree
       2. _____
           a. _____ Subheadings of third degree
           b. _____
               (1) _____ Subheadings of fourth degree
               (2) _____
                   (a) _____ Subheadings of fifth degree
                   (b) _____
   B. _____ Subheading of first degree

II. Second major heading

Each division must be in two parts. If you have a I level, you must have a II; if you have an A, you must have a B, and so forth. The degree to which you continue the subheads will depend, in part, upon the complexity of the subject. Subheads in a research paper seldom carry beyond the first series of small letters.

Writing a Formal Topic Outline

Build a topic outline with balanced phrases. The advantage of the topic outline is the speed with which you can develop it. Note this example that uses noun phrases:

I. Effects of television on children
   A. Vocabulary development
   B. Reading ability
   C. Visual arts appreciation
   D. Writing efficiency
   E. Discovery of technology
II. Effects of reading on children

The topic outline may also use gerund phrases ("Learning a vocabulary" and "Learning to read") or infinitive phrases ("To develop a vocabulary" or "To learn to read").

Writing a Formal Sentence Outline

The sentence outline requires full sentences for each heading and subheading. It has two advantages over the topic outline. First, many entries in a sentence outline can serve as topic sentences for paragraphs, thereby accelerating the writing process. Second, the subject/verb pattern establishes the logical direction of your thinking. (For example, the phrase "Vocabulary development" becomes "Television viewing can improve a child's vocabulary.") A portion of one writer's outline follows.

I. Television talk shows distort the truth.
  A. They skew objectivity and distort the truth.
    1. The producers and directors contrive an illusion of the truth.
    2. They are guilty of falsifying the line between fact and fiction.
  B. Viewers need to recognize television as a presentation, like a drama.
    1. Social reality is not a staple of television broadcasting.
    2. Viewers who abandon social reality buy into the sales pitch of television producers who promote both the show and the advertised products.

5d

The sentence outline identifies possible organizational problems rather than hiding them as a topic outline might do. The time devoted to writing a complete sentence outline will serve you well when you write the rough draft and revise it.

Finally, the finished paper should trace the issues, defend and support a thesis, and provide dynamic progression of issues and concepts that point forward to the conclusion. Each section of the paper should provide these elements:

- Identification of the problem or issue
- Analysis of the issues
- Presentation of evidence
- Interpretation and discussion of the findings

In every case you must generate the dynamics of the paper by (1) building anticipation in the introduction, (2) investigating the issues in the body, and (3) providing a final judgment. In this way, you will satisfy the demands of the academic reader who will expect you to examine a problem, cite some of the literature about it, and offer your ideas and interpretation of it.

All three are necessary in almost every instance. Consequently, your early organization will determine, in part, the success of your research paper.

6 Finding and Reading the Best Sources

The research paper tests your ability to find and cite appropriate and relevant sources. Thus, your task is twofold: (1) you must read and personally evaluate the sources for your own benefit as a writer, and (2) you must present them to your reader in your text as validated and authentic sources.

Therefore, this chapter offers tips about selecting and using the sources. It cuts to the heart of the matter: How do I find the best sources? Should I read all or just part of a source? How do I respond to it? The chapter also demonstrates how to write both an annotated bibliography and a review of the literature on a limited topic.

6a Identifying the Best Source Materials

Be skeptical about accepting every printed word as absolute. Constantly review and verify to your own satisfaction the words of your sources. This inverted pyramid shows a progression of excellent sources down to the less reliable sources. The chart does not ask you to ignore or dismiss items at the bottom, but it guides you as to when to feel confident and when to be cautious about the validity of the source.

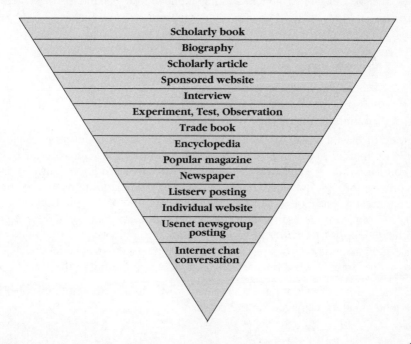

Scholarly book
Biography
Scholarly article
Sponsored website
Interview
Experiment, Test, Observation
Trade book
Encyclopedia
Popular magazine
Newspaper
Listserv posting
Individual website
Usenet newsgroup posting
Internet chat conversation

Use some of the following techniques for finding the most reliable sources.

Consulting with Your Instructor and the Librarians

Do not hesitate to ask your instructor or the librarians for help in finding sources. Instructors know the field, know the best writers, and can provide a brief list to get you started. Sometimes instructors will pull books from their office shelves to give you a starting point.

Librarians know the resources of the library. Their job is to serve your needs; never be afraid to ask for help.

Using Recent Sources

A book may look valuable, but if its copyright date is 1938, its content is suspect: time and new developments have probably passed it by (unless, of course, the work is a classic in its field). Scientific and technical topics always require up-to-date research. Learn to depend upon monthly and quarterly journals as well as books.

Evaluating Internet Sources

6a

The Internet supplies enormous amounts of material, some of it excellent and some not so good. You must make judgments about the validity and value of these materials. In addition to your common sense judgment, see the guidelines for evaluating Internet sources in 3d, page 30, and also the following checklist:

Determining the Validity of an Internet Site

- The site name will often reveal a serious and scholarly emphasis.
- The sponsor should be an institution or professional organization.
- The home page will reveal the nature and purpose of the site.
- Author/sponsor credentials will confirm the serious nature of the site.
- E-mail to an author or organization offers a means for scholarly query.

Using Journals Rather Than Magazines

Beware of biased reporting. In general, scholarly journals offer more reliable evidence than popular magazines. The authors of journals write for academic honour, and they research and document all sources. In addition, journal writers publish through university presses and academic organizations that require every article to pass the scrutiny of a jury of critics before its publication. An article about learning disabilities found in the *Canadian Journal of Education* or the *Journal of Learning Disabilities* should be reliable. An article about dyslexia in a Sunday newspaper or in a popular magazine may be less reliable.

Usually, but not in every case, you can identify a journal in these ways:

1. The journal does not have a colourful cover; in fact, the table of contents is often displayed on the cover.

2. There are no colourful graphics or photography to introduce each article, just a title and name of the author.
3. The word *journal* often appears in the title (e.g., *The Journal of Sociology*).
4. The yearly issues of a journal are bound into a book.
5. Usually, the pages of a journal are numbered continuously through all issues for a year (unlike magazines which are paginated anew with each issue).
6. The volume number and the page numbers are sufficient to find a journal article. You can best find a magazine article with day/month/year and the page numbers.
7. In general, journals are not issued as often as magazines.

Using Scholarly Books Rather Than Trade Books and Encyclopedias

Scholarly books, like journal articles, are subjected to careful review before publication. They are published because they give the very best treatment of a subject. Scholarly books, including textbooks, treat academic topics with in-depth discussions and careful documentation of the evidence. A college or university library is a repository for scholarly books—technical and scientific works, doctoral dissertations, publications of the university presses, and many textbooks.

6a

Trade books seldom treat with depth any scholarly subject. *How to Launch a Small Business* or *Landscaping with Rocks* are typical titles of non-fiction trade books found in bookstores, but not in college or university libraries (although public libraries often have vast holdings of trade books).

Encyclopedias, by design, contain brief surveys of every well-known person, event, place, and accomplishment. They will serve you well during preliminary investigation, but most instructors prefer that you go beyond encyclopedias to cite from scholarly books and journal articles.

Using Biographies to Evaluate an Author

You may need to search out information about an author to verify the standing and reputation of somebody that you want to paraphrase or quote in your paper. You may also need to discuss a creative writer's life in relation to his or her work. Or, you may wish to provide biographical details in your introduction.

You can learn about writers and their work on the Internet or in printed biographies. At a search engine, such as *Google,* just type in the name of an author and see what develops. The best writers will usually have several sites containing articles by and about them.

The librarian can help you find appropriate printed works, such as these:

Contemporary Authors, a set of biographies on contemporary writers
Dictionary of Canadian Biography, a review of writers and important figures in Canadian history
Who's Who in Philosophy, a list and discussion of the best writers and thinkers in the field

You can find reference works similar to these three books for almost every field.

Conducting a Citation Search

A citation search uncovers the authors whose works have been cited repeatedly in the literature. The process is fairly simple: (1) search several bibliographies of articles that treat your topic, (2) look for authors who are listed more than once, and (3) mark these names. The implication is that these authors, because they are cited often, must be experts in the field. The authors become *must* reading for you. The sources themselves will suggest a few important books and articles. For example, if you see the name "Gerald Friesen" listed repeatedly in the selected bibliographies, then you should read some of his material.

Three citation indexes will do some of this work for you:

Arts and Humanities Citation Index (AHCI) 1977–date
Science Citation Index (SCI) 1961–date
Social Sciences Citation Index (SSCI) 1966–date

Examining the Book Reviews

Whenever one book serves as the cornerstone for your research, you can test its critical reputation by reading a review or two. Two works provide summaries and critical points of view:

Canadian Book Review Annual (CBRA). Toronto: J. M. Wilson, 1975–date. www.interlog.com/~cbra/home.html

The Booklist. Chicago: American Library Assn., 1905–date. www. ala.org/booklist

To find other reviews, use one of the following indexes:

Book Review Index. Detroit: Gale, bimonthly. This work indexes reviews in 500 periodicals and newspapers. http://library.dialog. com/bluesheets/html/bl0137.html

Index to Book Reviews in the Humanities. Williamston, Michigan: Phillip Thompson, annually.

6b Reading All or Part of a Source

Confronted by several books and articles, many writers have trouble determining the value of material and the contribution it will make to the research paper. To save time, you must be selective in your reading. To serve your reader, you must cite carefully selected material that is pertinent to the argument. You cannot just insert huge blocks of quotation into the paper because you will lose your voice as the writer.

Evaluating an Article

1. The **title.** Look for code words that have relevance to your topic before you start reading the article. For example, *Children and Parents* may look ideal for child abuse research until you read the subtitle: *Children and Parents: Growing Up in New Guinea*.

2. An **abstract.** Reading an abstract is the best way to determine if an essay or a book will serve your specific needs. If an abstract is available

in a CD-ROM database or an abstracting service (e.g., *Psychological Abstracts*), read it before searching for the printed article. In like manner, if a printed article is preceded by an abstract, read the abstract first.

3. The **opening paragraphs.** If the opening of an article shows no relevance to your study, abandon it.

4. The **topic sentence** of each paragraph of the body. These first sentences of each paragraph will give you a digest of the author's main points.

5. The **closing paragraphs.** If the opening of an article seems promising, read the closing for relevance. Read the entire article only if this survey encourages you.

6. **Author credits.** Learn something about the credentials of the author. Magazine articles often provide brief biographical profiles of authors. The backs of book jackets often do the same. Even journal articles will include the author's academic affiliation and some credits. Internet home pages provide the same sort of information.

Evaluating a Book

A **book** requires you to examine several additional items:

1. A **table of contents.** A book's table of contents may reveal chapters that deal directly with your topic. Often, only one chapter is useful. For example, *Social Change and Education in Canada,* edited by Ghosh and Ray, has one chapter by Romulo Magsino devoted to parents' and children's rights. If you are researching this topic, then you should focus on this chapter, not the entire book.

2. A **book jacket,** if one is available. For example, the jacket to Ghosh and Ray's book says:

   With updated references and research, the third edition of *Social Change and Education in Canada* focusses on the rights of diverse communities to be served by the political system and on the policies devoted to protecting these rights.

   Such information can stimulate your reading and note taking from this important book.

3. The **foreword, preface, or introduction.** The preface often serves as a critical overview of the entire book, pinpointing the primary subject of the text and the particular approach of the author or editor. Read the preface to find a statement of purpose or the perspective of the author or editor on the subject. For example, Ghosh and Ray say in their preface:

   The authors of this book are broadly representative of Canada's regions and are nationally recognized for their scholarship in their particular fields. . . . The structure and approach of *Social Change and Education in Canada* provide the reader with a systematic overview, rather than a theoretical critique, of the relationship between social change and education in this country.

Such an introduction shows the scholarship and scope of the book.

4. The **index.** A book's index will list names and terminology with page numbers for all items mentioned within the text. The index, by virtue of its detailed listing, determines the relevance of the book to your research.

6c Responding to the Sources

After you find source material relevant to your subject, you must respond in several ways:

1. Read the material.
2. As you read, write notes that record key ideas.
3. Write notations on the margins of photocopied materials.
4. Outline the key ideas of an article.
5. Write a summary of the whole article.
6. Identify source information and relevant page numbers.

6c

Selecting Key Ideas for Your Notes

In many instances you may borrow only one idea from a source, one that you can rephrase into your own words. One student found this passage in an article by Jayson Myers in *Canadian Business*:

Home Ain't Where the Hope Is

Why are more and more Canadians heading south to work? . . . The real explanations are personal and economic. Take salaries. In the U.S. they are generally higher, and they are becoming more and more attractive every cent the Canadian dollar falls. Compare some of the starting salaries for graduate students offered this year by an information technology company with operations on both sides of the border. (All figures are in Canadian dollars.) A systems engineer could expect to make $50 000 in Canada, $64 000 in the U.S. . . . An MBA would start at $48 000 in Canada, $68 000 in the U.S.

Then there are taxes. At 53%, Canada's marginal personal income-tax rate is one of the highest in the world. Canadians hit that rate when their taxable income reaches $63 000. In the U.S., the top marginal rate is approximately 43% and it kicks in when income rises to $380 000 (Cdn). Capital gains are also taxed at a lower rate in the U.S., making shares and stock options more attractive.

A third factor has nothing to do with salaries or taxes. Rather, it's the range and depth of career opportunities. The sheer concentration of highly skilled workers in U.S. industry and the high number of job vacancies give the U.S. a distinct advantage.

Rather than copy the entire piece, the researcher read first, found the passage related to her thesis and outline, and wrote this note:

> **From "Home Ain't Where the Hope Is," page 1**
> Both personal income and capital gains tax rates are much higher in Canada than in the U.S.

The writer has selected only a small portion of the text for her notes to compare U.S. and Canadian tax rates.

Outlining the Key Ideas of a Source

Most books have a table of contents that outlines the basic ingredients of the book. Consult it for issues that deserve your critical reading. In the case of an essay, you can frame your own outline to capture an author's primary themes; that is, list the main ideas and subtopics (1) to show the hierarchy of issues, (2) to identify parallel parts, and (3) to locate supporting ideas. The goal is to discover the author's primary and secondary ideas. The outline of the "Home Ain't Where the Hope Is" passage, above, might look like this:

6c

> **Home Ain't Where the Hope Is**
>   Why Canadian workers head south to the U.S.
>   Salaries higher in U.S. as Canadian dollar declines
>   Systems engineer starts at $14 000 higher in U.S.
>   MBA starts at $20 000 higher in U.S.
>   Taxes lower in U.S.
>   Marginal personal income tax rate 10 percent lower in U.S.
>   Marginal personal income tax rate begins in Canada at $63 000
>   Marginal personal income tax rate begins in U.S. at $380 000
>   Career opportunities
>   Higher demand in U.S. for skilled workers
>   Higher job vacancy rate in U.S.

Such an outline gives the researcher a clear overview of the issues. It also provides the basic ingredients for a summary note card, as demonstrated below in "Writing a Summary or a Précis."

Writing a Summary or a Précis

A *summary* condenses into a brief note the general nature of a source. In some cases you might use the summary in your paper, but more than anything else it serves to remind you later on about the source's relevance to your study. Note this example of a summary:

> **From "Home Ain't Where the Hope Is," page 1**
> Economic and personal motives lure Canadian workers south to the U.S. where salaries are higher, taxes are lower, and career opportunities are more varied and plentiful.

A *précis* is a highly polished summary that you can transfer to your paper or use in an annotated bibliography. It often uses direct quotation from the original source, as in the following example.

> **From "Home Ain't Where the Hope Is," page 1**
> "Home Ain't Where the Hope Is" indicates that both economic and personal motives lure Canadians south to the U.S. job market. U.S. salaries are "generally higher," sometimes by as much as $20 000 for starting graduates. Both U.S. personal income and capital gains taxes are lower, and U.S. career opportunities offer "a distinct advantage" in their number and variety.

Compare the above summary and précis and note the differences. For further details and examples, see 7e "Writing Summary Notes and Précis Notes," pages 62–63.

6d Selecting a Mix of Both Primary and Secondary Sources

6d

Primary Sources

Primary sources are the original words of a writer, such as a novel, speech, eyewitness account, letter, autobiography, interview, or the written report of original research. Feel free to quote often from a primary source when it has direct relevance to your discussion. If you examine a poem by Dylan Thomas, you must quote the poem. If you examine Jean Chrétien's domestic policies on health care, you must quote from federal government documents. The best evidence you can offer when writing about a poem, story, novel, or drama will be the words of the author. Therefore, quote often from these works to defend the thesis of a literary paper. The same is true with a history paper where you should cite the words of the key figure, whether it be Sir John A. Macdonald, Marie Antoinette, or Karl Marx.

In the social sciences, your best evidence will be found in the wording of original case studies and reports of social workers and psychiatrists. In a similar fashion, education will offer test data, interviews, pilot studies, and other forms of primary information. Thus, every discipline will offer you plenty of primary source material, as shown on page 51.

Secondary Sources

Secondary sources are writings *about* the primary sources and *about* the authors who produce them. Examples of secondary sources are a report on a presidential speech, a review of new scientific findings, or an analysis of the imagery of a poem. A biography provides a second-hand view of the life of a notable person. A history book interprets events. These evaluations, analyses, or interpretations provide ways of looking at original, primary sources. You should cite secondary sources to review the literature on the subject. For example, your study of cloning will need a survey of opinions about the procedure, not merely data on how it's done. Your examination of Brian Mulroney's performance as prime minister of Canada will need more than his words; you will want a survey of historians and their points of view.

  Do not quote too liberally from secondary sources. Be selective. Use a well-worded sentence, not the entire paragraph. Work a key phrase into your text, not eight or nine lines. (See "Selecting Key Ideas for Your Notes," pages 48–49.)

  The subject of a research paper determines in part the nature of the source materials. Use the following chart as a guide.

Primary and Secondary Sources by Discipline

	Primary Sources	*Secondary Sources*
Literature	Novels, poems, plays, short stories, letters, diaries, manuscripts, autobiographies, films, videos of live performances	Journal articles, reviews, biographies, critical books about writers and their works
Government, Political Science, and History	Speeches and writings by political and historical figures, government reports, and reports of agencies and departments	Newspaper reports, news magazines, political journals and newsletters, journal articles, and history books
Social Sciences	Case studies, findings from surveys and questionnaires; reports of social workers, psychiatrists, and lab technicians	Commentary and evaluations in reports, documents, journal articles, and books
Sciences	Tools and methods, experiments, findings from tests and experiments, observations, discoveries, and test patterns	Interpretations and discussions of test data as found in journals and books (scientific books, which are quickly dated, are less valuable than up-to-date journals)
Fine Arts	Films, paintings, music, sculptures as well as reproductions and synopses of these for research purposes about the authors and their works	Evaluations in journal articles, critical reviews, biographies, and critical books
Business	Market research and testing, technical studies and investigations, drawings, designs, models, memoranda and letters, computer data	Discussion of the business world in newspapers, business magazines, journals, government documents, and books
Education	Pilot studies, term projects, sampling results, tests and test data, surveys, interviews, observations, statistics, and computer data	Analysis and evaluation of educational experimentation in journals, pamphlets, books, and reports

6d

6e Preparing An Annotated Bibliography

An *annotation* is a summary of the contents of a book or article. A *bibliography* is a list of sources on a selected topic. Thus, an annotated bibliography does two important things: (1) it gives a bibliographic entry to all your sources, and (2) it summarizes the contents of each book or article. Writing an annotated bibliography may at first appear to be busywork, but it will evaluate the strength of your sources.

- For instructions on writing an annotation, see 7e, page 63.
- For instructions on writing the citation to a source in MLA style, see Chapter 9. For other styles, consult Chapters 10–12.

The next example demonstrates an annotated bibliography, in MLA style, of Internet and print sources on the issue of the Canadian brain drain.

6e

Smythe 1

Annotated Bibliography

Dubé, Jean. "Federal Conservative Party Vows to Plug Brain Drain to US." <u>Hill-Times</u> 6 Nov. 2000: 27. This article by the Tory human resources critic outlines the federal Conservative Party's "three-pronged approach" to stemming Canada's brain drain by increasing post-secondary funding, introducing an "income contingent" loan repayment program, and legislating a tax credit based on loan repayment.

Frank, Jeff, and Eric Beliar, eds. <u>South of the Border: Graduates from the Class of '95 Who Moved to the United States</u>. Quebec: Human Resources Development Canada, 1999. This report presents results from a survey by Human Resources Development Canada and Statistics Canada of 1995 graduates who moved to the United States. Data was collected on personal characteristics, reasons for relocating to the U.S., education and work experience, and future plans.

Myers, Jayson. "Home Ain't Where the Hope Is: Plugging the Brain Drain to the U.S." <u>Canadian Business</u> 11 Dec. 1998: 104. This brief article indicates that both economic and personal motives lure Canadians south to the U.S. job market. U.S. salaries are "generally higher", both U.S. personal income and capital gains taxes are lower, and U.S. career opportunities offer "a distinct advantage" in their number and variety.

Steffler, Jason. <u>The Canadian's Guide to the Brain Drain FAQ</u>. 2001. 25 July 2001 <www.magma.ca/~jagwar/ cdnGuideBrainDrain/cdnGuideBrainDrainBase.html>. This online guide answers questions frequently asked by Canadians who are considering employment in the U.S. Topics include visas, work permits, taxes, salaries, and benefits.

6f Preparing a Review of the Literature on a Topic

The review of literature presents a set of summaries in essay form for two purposes. First, it helps you investigate the topic because it forces you to examine and then to show how each source addresses the problem. Hence, it should not simply list summaries of the sources without relating each source to your thesis. Also, it organizes and classifies the sources for the benefit of the reader.

The following brief literature review, written in MLA style, classifies the sources with respect to three possible causes of the Canadian brain drain: low salaries, high taxes, and lack of challenging career opportunities in Canada. With this analysis, the research paper will be easier to write, and the instructor, who may request such a literature review, will see that the project is moving in the right direction.

Remember that most professors will require a title page and a running head. (See "Running Heads," Appendix, page 173, 9d, "Formatting the Paper in MLA Style," page 110, and the sample paper in 9e, pages 112–117.)

Sinclair 1

6f

The Exhaustion of Canada's Human Resources:
Literature Review

by
Jennifer Sinclair

99.111 Introduction to University
Dr. C. A. Butterill
March 25, 2002

Sinclair 2

Canada continues to experience a bitter brain drain, as many skilled individuals relocate to the United States, where their expertise is more likely to be acknowledged and appreciated. The exodus of valuable human capital out of Canada can be attributed to unattractive Canadian salaries, high income taxes, and the lack of challenging career opportunities in Canada compared with countries such as the United States.

Salaries

According to Ian Jack (E8), salaries in the United States are generally higher than those offered in Canada for the same level of experience and education, and therefore Canada is finding it harder to hold on to its own professionals. Jayson Myers claims that graduates in professional fields can make up to $20 000 more in the United States, and that this figure is even more appealing in light of the falling

Sinclair 3

Canadian dollar (104). A 1999 survey by Statistics Canada indicates that 1.5 percent of the students who graduated from a Canadian post-secondary institution in 1995 relocated to the United States (Frank and Beliar 35). Although skeptics argue that 1.5 percent is an insignificant number, most of these 4600 graduates were at the top of their graduating class, had master's degrees or Ph.D.'s, and "tended to be high quality people in certain key fields" (Frank and Beliar 36). A study by Don DeVoretz confirms that the majority of Canadian emigrants drawn to the United States in pursuit of higher salaries are highly educated, with 17 percent being Ph.D. graduates ("Canada's Brain Drain"). Increasing tuition costs, which leave graduates with a high debt load, are an added incentive to seek higher paid employment south of the border (Hodder 16). Jean Dubé, the federal Conservative human resources critic observes:

> Too often, students are graduating owing student loans totalling in the neighbourhood of $40 000. No wonder graduates are tempted to leave Canada for higher salaries elsewhere, [if] for no other reason than to pay off their student loans. (27)

Taxes

Many people are convinced that high income taxes in Canada take away initiatives to be successful and simply drive a significant number of people out of the country. Myers states: "At 53%, Canada's marginal personal income-tax rate is one of the highest in the world" (104). As well, the Canadian system of taxation dramatically penalizes Canadians as their incomes increase (Steffler), and U.S. tax brackets are much larger; thus, to reach the next highest rate, taxable income must increase substantially (Jack E8, Myers 104).

Career Opportunities

Opportunities for challenging careers and professional development in specialized fields of study are appealing to Canadian emigrants (Frank and Beliar 36), which puts Canada at a great disadvantage considering that Canadian taxpayers have in part funded the emigrants' education (Jack E8). A "one-year outflow of taxpayer-financed human capital is the equivalent of 2.5 years of Simon Fraser University's 1996–97 operating budget" for its "15,000 students" (DeVoretz and Laryea 17).

Conclusion

Jean Dubé emphasizes that "the brain drain is not a myth; it is real" (27). According to Henry Ramer, the exodus of Canada's human resources proves that "success is more important than allegiance," and Canada must accept the new era's technological changes and increase support for those individuals with innovative ideas that will lead to economic prosperity for Canada in the 21st century.

6f

Sinclair 4

Sources Cited

"Canada's Brain Drain." Narr. Henry Ramer. Global Television. CKND, Winnipeg. 22 Nov. 1999.

DeVoretz, Don, and Samuel A. Laryea. <u>Canadian Human Capital Transfers: The United States and Beyond</u>. Toronto: C. D. Howe Institute, 1998.

Dubé, Jean. "Federal Conservative Party Vows to Plug Brain Drain to US." <u>Hill-Times</u> 6 Nov. 2000: 27.

Frank, Jeff, and Eric Beliar, eds. <u>South of the Border: Graduates from the Class of '95 Who Moved to the United States</u>. Quebec: Human Resources Development Canada, 1999.

Hodder, Harvey. "Under-funding of Post-Secondary Educational Institutions." <u>Canadian Parliamentary Review</u> 23.4 (2000): 15–16.

Jack, Ian. "The Brain Drain to the U.S. Is Real and Costly." <u>National Post</u> 17 Apr. 1999: E8.

Myers, Jayson. "Home Ain't Where the Hope Is: Plugging the Brain Drain to the U.S." <u>Canadian Business</u> 11 Dec. 1998: 104.

Steffler, Jason. <u>The Canadian's Guide to the Brain Drain FAQ</u>. 2001. 25 July 2001 <www.magma.ca/~jagwar/cdnGuideBrainDrain/cdnGuideBrainDrainBase.html>.

6f

Note that the "Sources Cited" list goes on its own separate page and that the writer has selected a variety of both print and electronic sources (i.e., a book, journal articles, articles from a reputable magazine and newspaper, a government document, a television program, and a website).

7 Writing Notes and Working with Source Material

Scholarship is the sharing of information. The primary reason for any research paper is to announce and publicize new findings:

- the details of a study of the wild grizzly bears of British Columbia's Khutzeymateen Valley
- the results of cancer research
- the findings of a two-year pilot study of diversified farming in the Prairie provinces.

Similarly, you must explain your findings from a geology field trip, disclose research on illegal dumping of medical waste, or discuss the results of an investigation into overcrowding of school classrooms. You will often support your position by citing the experts in the field, so accuracy in your quotations and paraphrases is essential.

7a Creating Effective Notes

You will need to write notes of high quality so they fit appropriate places in your outline, as discussed in Chapter 5. In addition, you will need to write different types of notes that reflect your evaluation of the sources—quotations for well-phrased passages by authorities but paraphrased or summarized notes for less notable materials. Therefore, consider the following strategies for taking notes (each is explained fully in this chapter):

- *Personal notes* (7b) that express each of your own ideas so you will have a substantial body of individual concepts, not merely a set of borrowed viewpoints or a string of borrowed quotations.
- *Quotation notes* (7c) that reproduce the wisdom and distinguished language of an authority.
- *Paraphrased notes* (7d) that interpret and restate in your own words what the authority has said.
- *Summary notes* (7e) that provide a quick overview of factual data that has marginal value.
- *Précis notes* (7e)) that capture the essence of one writer's ideas in capsule form. This type includes the plot summary, the review note, the abstract, and the annotation to a bibliography entry.
- *Field notes* (7f) that keep an accurate record of interviews, questionnaire tabulations, lab experiments, and various types of field research.

Note: The Internet now offers many articles that you can print or download to a file. Treat these as you would a printed source; that is, develop notes from them that you can transfer into your draft.

Whether you write your notes by word processing or by hand, you should keep in mind some basic rules:

Tips for Creating Effective Notes

1. *Write one item per note.* One item of information on each note aids shuffling and rearranging the data during all stages of organization. On a computer, make single files for each note or one file with notes labelled and recorded for easy retrieval.

2. *List the source.* Make it a practice to list name, year, and page number on your notes; then you will be ready to make in-text citations for MLA, APA, or other academic styles. Abbreviate the exact source (e.g., "Thornton 431" for MLA or "Smith, 1997, p. 62" for APA) to serve as a quick reference to the full citation.

3. *Label each note.* To help arrange your notes, you should (1) describe each (e.g., "objectivity on television") or (2) put one of your outline headings on each (e.g., "Television as a presentation").

4. *Write a full note.* When you have a source in your hands, write full, well-developed sentences to speed the writing of your first draft. They may require editing later to fit the context of your draft. Avoid photo-copying everything because the writing will remain to be done later.

5. *Keep everything.* Try to save every card, sheet, scrap, and note to authenticate a date, age, page number, or full name.

6. *Label your personal notes.* To distinguish your thoughts from those of authorities, label personal ideas with "PER" (personal note), "my idea," "mine," or "personal note."

Conforming to the Conventions of Research Style

Your note taking will be more effective from the start if you practise the conventions of style for citing sources within your text (termed in-text citations). Write your notes to conform to your discipline—MLA, APA, CBE, CMS (Chicago)—as shown briefly below and explained in detail in chapters 9, 10, 11, and 12.

Form of In-Text Citations

MLA: Lawrence Smith comments, "The suicidal teen causes severe damage to the psychological condition of peers" (34).

APA: Smith (1997) commented, "The suicidal teen causes severe damage to the psychological condition of peers" (p. 34).

CBE Number: Smith (4) has commented, "The suicidal teen causes severe damage to the psychological condition of peers."

CMS (Chicago): Lawrence Smith comments, "The suicidal teen causes severe damage to the psychological condition of peers."[3]

These styles will be displayed throughout this chapter, clearly labelled in every example.

7a

Using a Computer for Note Taking

The computer affects note-taking strategies in several ways:

1. You can enter your notes into the word processor using one of two methods:

    a. Write each note as a separate temporary file under a common directory so each note can be moved later into the appropriate section of your TEXT file by a COPY, READ, or INSERT command. In other words, create a directory (e.g., FAULKNER). Then write separate files, each with a distinctive title (e.g., WATSON [a critic], SNOPES [a character], or GREED [an issue]. Periodically, print these notes on paper for safety and editing purposes. Or:

    b. Write all notes into a single file, labelled with a short title, such as NOTES. With this method, your notes will be gathered in *one* file, not numerous ones. It is advisable to give each new note a code word or title. When you begin writing the paper, you merely open this same file of notes and begin writing at the top of the file, which will push the notes down as you write. When you need one of your notes, you can use FIND or SEARCH with the code words, or you can scan down through the file to find the appropriate note. With this method, you can move your notes easily within the one document by CUT and PASTE or BLOCK and COPY commands; you can transfer notes quickly into your text. Printing the notes on paper before beginning your writing will provide reference points for your work.

2. Computer notes, once typed, will not need retyping. You need only move the note into your rough draft and then revise it to fit the context. (See 9a, 10c, 11a, and 12a, "Blending Sources into Your Writing.")

3. You can record the bibliographic information for each source by listing it in a BIBLIO file to build the necessary list of references in one alphabetical file. Chapters 9, 10, 11, and 12 show the correct forms.

Developing Hand-Written Notes

Hand-written cards should conform to these additional conventions:

1. *Use ink.* Write notes legibly in ink because pencilled notes become blurred after repeated shuffling of the cards.

2. If you are writing by hand, *use two sizes* or *two colours of index cards,* one for notes and one for bibliography entries. This practice keeps the two separate.

3. *Write on one side of a card.* Material on the back of a card may be overlooked. Staple two or more cards used for one note.

7b Writing Personal Notes

During your research, record *your* thoughts on the issues by writing plenty of personal notes. Personal notes and writing in a research journal are essential. Personal notes allow you to record your discoveries, to reflect on the findings, to make connections, to explore another point of view, and to identify prevailing views and patterns of thought.

Remember, the content of a research paper is not a collection of ideas transmitted by experts in books and articles; it is an expression of your ideas as supported by the scholarly evidence. Readers are primarily interested in *your* thesis statement, *your* topic sentences, and *your* fresh view of the issues. Personal notes should conform to these standards:

Standards for Personal Notes

1. The idea on the note is exclusively yours.
2. The note is labelled with "my idea," "mine," "personal thought"; later you can be certain that it has not been borrowed.
3. The note can be a rough summary, an abstract sketch of ideas, or a complete sentence or two. Most personal notes will need to be revised later when you draft the paper.
4. The note lists other authorities who address this same issue.
5. The jottings in your research journal are original and not copied from the sources.

Two samples of personal notes follow:

My note

———

Mike Bullard, Vicki Gabereau, Oprah Winfrey, and all the others will sometimes uncover a bit of truth out of the people interviewed, but any sense of objectivity goes out the window.

My note

———

Objectivity on television, if it exists at all, gets skewed out of shape by forces within the television world as well as forces acting on the world of communication.

7c Writing Direct Quotation Notes

You must adhere to a few rules when copying the words of another person:

Rules for Writing Direct Quotation Notes

1. Select quotations that are important and well-phrased but not trivial or commonly known. Do not quote, for example, "Joy Kogawa['s] . . . 1981 novel, *Obasan,* dealt with her family's internment" (Finkel and Conrad 310). Instead, quote (in MLA style):

   "Kogawa's fiction makes such grievous wrong from the past a presence still" (Moss 201).

2. Use quotation marks. Do not copy the words of a source into your paper in such a way that readers will think *you* wrote the material.
3. Use the exact phrasing of the source, including the author's punctuation.
4. Provide an in-text citation to the author and page number, as shown by this note in APA style:

> Pungente and O'Malley (1999) stress that media education prevents television viewers from being like the cave people of Plato's *Republic* for whom "reality is nothing but the shadows of the objects [on the cave wall] and the voices that accompany them" (p. 20).

5. Place the page citation *outside* the final quotation mark but *inside* the period.
6. Write notes from both primary sources (original words by a writer or speaker) and secondary sources (comments after the fact about original works). (See 6d, "Selecting a Mix of Both Primary and Secondary Sources," pages 50–51.)
7. Try to quote key phrases, sentences, and short passages, not entire paragraphs. Find the essential statement and feature it; do not force your reader to journey through a long quoted passage in search of the relevant statement. Make the quotation a part of your work, as in this example in CMS note style:

> Tabloid television is not merely the news as much as it is entertainment. For example, one source notes that "the networks live by the dictum 'keep it short and to the point'" so they make the news "lively."[1]

7d

7d Writing Paraphrased Notes

A paraphrase requires you to restate in your own words the thought, meaning, and attitude of someone else. The paraphrase maintains the sound of your voice, sustains your style, and avoids an endless string of direct quotations. A paraphrase both interprets and rewrites. With *interpretation* you act as a bridge between the source and the reader as you capture the wisdom of the source in approximately the same number of words. Your *rewriting,* developed by careful reading and evaluation of the sources, requires you to (1) name the source, (2) indicate the source's approach to the issue (e.g., positive, negative, ironic), and (3) rewrite the material, as shown here in MLA style:

> One writer urges the use of fluoride in all drinking water (Smythe 16).

Keep in mind these rules for paraphrasing.

Rules for Writing Paraphrased Notes

1. Rewrite the original in about the same number of words.
2. Provide an in-text citation to the source.
3. Retain exceptional words and phrases from the original by enclosing them within quotation marks.

4. Preserve the tone of the original by suggesting moods of satire, humour, doubt, and so on. Do this by showing the author's attitude with your verbs: "Edward Zigler *condemns . . . defends . . . argues . . . explains . . . humorously observes . . . defines.*"

Here are examples (in APA style) that show the differences between a quotation note and a paraphrased one.

Short Quotation

Heredity   Hein 294

———

Hein (2001) explains, "Except for identical twins, each person's heredity is unique" (p. 294).

Short Paraphrased Note

Heredity   Hein 294

———

Hein (2001) explains that heredity is special and distinct for each of us, unless a person is an identical twin (p. 294).

Long Quotation

Heredity   Hein 294

———

Hein (2001) clarifies the phenomenon:

> Since only half of each parent's chromosomes are transmitted to a child and since this half represents a chance selection of those the child could inherit, only twins that develop from a single fertilized egg that splits in two have identical chromosomes. (p. 294)

Note: See 9b, page 90, and 10c, page 119, for more information on long quotations in MLA and APA styles.

Long Paraphrased Note

Heredity   Hein 294

———

Hein (2001) specifies that twins have identical chromosomes because they grow from one egg that divides after it has been fertilized. He affirms that most brothers and sisters differ because of the "chance selection" of chromosomes transmitted by each parent (p. 294).

To repeat, paraphrasing keeps the length of the note about the same as the original but converts the original into your language and style. Any specific wording of the source is placed within quotation marks.

7d

> *Caution:* Put the source aside while paraphrasing to avoid copying word for word. Return to the source for comparison of the finished paraphrase with the source to be certain that the paraphrase truly rewrites the original and that the paraphrase uses quotation marks with any phrasing or key words retained from the source.

7e Writing Summary Notes and Précis Notes

You may write two types of summary notes. One is a quick sketch of the material and the other is the more carefully drawn précis.

Summary Notes

The typical **summary note** represents borderline information for your study. It briefly profiles the material without great concern for style or expression. Your purpose at the moment will be quick, concise writing without careful wording. Reduce a long paragraph into a sentence, tighten an article into a brief paragraph, and summarize a book into a page. If the information is needed, you can rewrite the note later in a clear, appropriate prose style and, if necessary, return to the source for revision. Use summary notes for several types of information:

1. Source material that appears to have marginal value
2. Facts that do not fit a code word or an outline heading
3. Statistics that have questionable value for your study
4. The interesting position of a source speaking on a closely related subject but not on your specific topic
5. A reference to several works that address the same issue, as shown in this example in CMS note style:

   Media education has been examined in books by Bianculli,[1] Pungente and O'Malley,[2] and Stark,[3] and in articles by Chidle,[4] and Salutin.[5]

6. A summary note needs documentation to the author and page number, but a page number is unnecessary when your note summarizes the entire book or article, not a specific passage.

Précis Notes

A **précis note** differs from the quick summary. It serves a specific purpose, so it deserves a polished style for transfer into the paper. Note this example, in which the writer has précised a seven-page section of a fact sheet in three sentences.

The CRTC Factsheet indicates that in the 1990s considerable progress was made in addressing the controversial issue of television violence. In Canada advocates of free speech and supporters of censorship adopted a "cooperative, consensual approach." This led to mandated industry codes, program classification, increased public awareness, and more media literacy initiatives.

The next précis note reviews two entire articles in only a few words.

Steven McClellan has two closely related articles on this subject, but both are about the proliferation of talk shows. He opens both with "Talk, Talk, Talk."

Using the Précis to Write an Annotated Bibliography

An annotation is a sentence or paragraph that offers explanatory or critical commentary on an article or book. The précis can serve you in this case because it explains the contents of a source. See samples in 6e, page 52.

Using the Précis as the Form for an Abstract

An abstract is a brief description that appears at the beginning of an article. It is, in truth, a précis. Usually, it is written by the article's author, and it helps readers make decisions about reading or skipping the article. You will find entire volumes devoted to abstracts, such as *Psychological Abstracts* or *Abstracts of English Studies.* See 10e, page 129, and 10f, page 130, for the use of the abstract in a paper written in APA style.

7f Writing Notes from Field Research

You will be expected to conduct field research in some instances. This work will require different kinds of notes kept on charts, cards, note pads, laboratory notebooks, a research journal, or the computer.

If you **interview** knowledgeable people, make careful notes during the interview and, perhaps, transcribe those notes to your computer in a more polished form. A tape recorder can serve as a backup to your note taking; however, be sure to get permission from the persons involved.

If you conduct a **questionnaire,** the results will become valuable data for developing notes, graphs, and charts for your research paper.

If you conduct **experiments** and **tests** and **measurements,** the findings serve as your notes for the "results" section of the report and will give you the basis for the "discussion" section. (See 4e, page 34 for a full discussion of the four parts to a report of empirical research.)

7g

7g Avoiding Plagiarism

Plagiarism (purposely using another person's writing as your own) is a serious breach of ethics. Knowledgeable, ethical behaviour is necessary whenever you handle sources and cite the words of other people.

Documenting Your Sources for a Purpose

Blending the sources into your text is a major part of the research paper assignment, as explained in great detail in chapters 9 (MLA), 10 (APA), 11 (CBE), and 12 (CMS). You will display academic integrity if you cite borrowed ideas, quote a well-worded phrase with appropriate credit to the speaker, and summarize the best ideas on a topic as expressed by several of the best minds (provided again that you name them).

Research writing is an exercise in critical thinking that tests your ability to assimilate ideas and then to disseminate them in a clear, logical progression. Therefore, one of your roles as researcher is to share with the reader the fundamental scholarship on a narrow topic. You will explain, not merely the subject, but also the *literature* of the topic. Rather than secretly stuffing your paper with plagiarized materials, announce boldly the name of your sources to let readers know the scope of your reading on the subject, as in this note in MLA style.

Government action during the October Crisis

    ————

Commenting on political activities during the October Crisis of 1970, Denis Smith makes this observation in his text, <u>Bleeding Hearts . . . Bleeding Country: Canada and the Quebec Crisis</u>: "I was an opponent of the response to terror chosen by the governments of Canada and Quebec. I remain an opponent. [. . .] What is important to me now is that we should not compound the errors of 1970 and fall deeper into political folly" (xiv).

This sentence allows the reader to identify the writer's voice and the words of the source. It gives clear evidence of the writer's investigation into the subject. It is intellectually honest. *Note:* When instructors see an in-text citation but no quotation marks, they will assume that you are paraphrasing, not quoting. Be sure that their assumption is true.

7g

Critical Thinking Tip

To avoid plagiarism, develop personal notes full of your own ideas on a topic. Discover how you think about the issue. Write a "baseline" paper, which is an essay of your ideas and thoughts *without* the use of any sources. Then, rather than copy sources onto your pages of text, try to synthesize the ideas of the authorities with your own thoughts by using the précis and the paraphrase. Rethink ideas after your reading, make meaningful connections, and when you refer to a specific source—as you inevitably will—give it credit and use quotation marks to enclose the exact wording of the source.

Understanding Plagiarism So You Can Avoid It

Fundamentally, the plagiarist offers the words or ideas of another person as his or her own. A major violation is the representation of another student's work as yours. Also flagrantly dishonest are those writers who knowingly use sources without documentation. These two instances of plagiarism are cause enough for failure in the course.

A grey area in plagiarism is carelessness that results in an error. For example, student writers fail to enclose quoted material within quotation marks, yet they provide an in-text citation (perhaps because the note card was mis-labelled or carelessly written); or the writer's paraphrase never quite becomes a paraphrase—too much of the original is left intact (see "Student Version A," page 67). Although these cases are not flagrant plagiarism, these students face the scrutiny of instructors who demand precision in citations. Admittedly, a double standard exists. Magazine writers and newspaper reporters quote people constantly without documentation. But academic writers must document original ideas borrowed from source materials. The reason goes back to the opening discussion. Each scholar builds upon previous scholarship. Your research in any area perpetuates a chain reaction. You begin where others leave off by borrowing from others and by advancing your findings and theory. Then somebody else, perhaps, will continue your research and carry it to another level. Without proper documentation on your part, the research will grind to a halt.

Consequently, you must conform to a few rules of conduct:

Rules for Avoiding Plagiarism

1. Let the reader know when you begin borrowing from a source by introducing the quotation or paraphrase with the name of the authority.
2. Enclose within quotation marks all quoted materials.
3. Make certain that paraphrased material has been rewritten into your own style and language. The simple rearrangement of sentence patterns is unacceptable.
4. Provide specific in-text documentation for each borrowed item.
5. Provide a bibliographic entry for every source cited in the paper.

7g

In short, quotation marks are an absolute *must* when using the exact words of someone else. Citing the page number to a source is good, yes, but you must also put quotation marks around a key word, a phrase, or a clause if the words are not your own.

Common Knowledge Exceptions

These are the rules, but facts available as common knowledge are exceptions. Even though you might read it in a source, you need not cite the fact that Nunavut is Canada's newest territory, that it has three regions, or that Iqaluit is the capital. Information of this sort requires *no* in-text citation, as shown in the following example.

> The name of Canada's newest territory, Nunavut, pronounced "Noo-na-voot" and written as <u>Nunavut </u>in both English and French, means "Our Land" in Inuktitut, the Inuit language. Nunavut's three regions are called Qikiqtaaluk (or Baffin), Kivalliq (or Keewatin), and Kitikmeot. Nunavut's capital is Iqaluit.

However, if you borrow specific ideas or exact wording from a source, especially information and statistics, you must provide an in-text citation to the source. The following example is in MLA style.

Inuit make up 80 percent of Nunavut's population; the remaining 20 percent are mostly people of British and European descent (Hancock 56).

Here are two more examples: the first needs no documentation, but the second (in MLA style) does because the opinion belongs to the source.

Written in 1930 by Charles Yale Harrison, <u>Generals Die in Bed</u> is a portrayal of the experiences of a group of Canadian soldiers in the First World War.

In <u>Generals Die in Bed</u>, Harrison presents combat with "a disarmingly bland directness that precludes moral reflection" (Moss 162).

Checklist for Common Knowledge Exceptions

- Would an intelligent person know this information?
- Did you know it before you discovered it in the source?
- Is it encyclopedia-type information?
- Has this information become general knowledge by being reported repeatedly in many different sources?

7g

Borrowing from a Source Correctly

The next two examples in MLA style will demonstrate the differences between genuine research writing and plagiarism. First is the original reference material, followed by two student versions. One demonstrates plagiarism and one does not.

Original Material from Two Sources

Researchers, as the National Film Board of Canada's notes for <u>Live TV</u> point out, . . . tell us that developing media literacy skills reduces TV's impact. The objective of media education is not to get kids to turn off TV, but to ask themselves: "Who is smarter—the TV or me?" (Pungente and O'Malley 122).

It has been said that the cumulative impact of indiscriminate viewing of violence is damaging to children because it "desensitizes" them to violence. Perhaps, but if this is true it is the result of watching television passively, uncritically, accepting its values as your own, having no criteria to discern the shoddy from the excellent, the intelligent from the stupid. In other words, lacking the critical thinking skills that come with media education (Pungente and O'Malley 114).

From John J. Pungente and Martin O'Malley, <u>More Than Meets the Eye: Watching Television Watching Us</u>, Toronto: McClelland and Stewart (1999): 114–122.

Student Version A (This paragraph is plagiarized and unacceptable)

The accumulative force of seeing TV violence is damaging to children because they become immune to the violence. This happens when they watch it casually, without criticism, agreeing with its values, with no bases to judge the good from the bad, the intelligent from the stupid. They lack the critical thinking skills that come with media education. Media literacy lessens the impact of TV on children. Children should not aim to turn off the TV, but rather question themselves: "Is it me or the TV who is smarter?" (Pungente and O'Malley 122).

Even though the sources' authors and one page number are shown at the end, this use of the two passages is plagiarized because it merely substitutes words for the original, misrepresents the two passages, does not reference each idea used, does not employ quotation marks for words used in the original, and does not mention the first page which supplies some of the words and ideas.

Student Version B (Acceptable)

Children can become desensitized to violence after long-term "indiscriminate" exposure to violence on TV. Pungente and O'Malley argue the desensitization occurs when the viewing is passive and without discernment (122). They point out that media education, however, can shape children's "media literacy skills" (114) and develop their "critical thinking skills" (122). Rather than turning off the TV, children will come to realize that they, not the TV, are the smart ones (114).

This version represents a satisfactory handling of the source material. The authorities are acknowledged near the outset of the borrowing, a key section has been paraphrased in the student's own words with a correct page citation to Pungente and O'Malley's book, and other parts have been quoted directly with page citations supplied. In summary, note these required instances for citing a source:

Required Instances for Citing a Source

Examples are in APA Style.

1. An original idea derived from a source, whether quoted or paraphrased:

   Genetic engineering, by which a child's body shape and intellectual ability are predetermined, raises memories of Nazi attempts in eugenics (Riddell, 2001, p. 19).

2. Your summary of original ideas by a source:

   Genetic engineering has been described as the rearrangement of the genetic structure in animals or in plants, which is a technique that takes a section of DNA and reattaches it to another section (Rosenthal, 2000, pp. 19–20).

3. Factual information that is not common knowledge:

Madigan (1999, p. 51) has shown that genetic engineering has its risks: a non-pathogenic organism might be converted into a pathogenic one or an undesirable trait might develop as a result of a mistake.

4. Any exact wording copied from a source:

Woodward (2000) asserts that genetic engineering is "a high stakes moral rumble that involves billions of dollars and affects the future" (p. 68).

7g

8 Drafting the Paper in an Academic Style

As you draft your paper, you should adopt an academic style that reflects your discipline, as discussed in 8a. Present a fair, balanced treatment of the subject. Mentioning opposing viewpoints early in a paper gives you something to work against and may strengthen your conclusion. Your early draft is a time for discovery. Later, during the revision period, you can strengthen skimpy paragraphs, refine your prose, and rearrange material to maintain the momentum of your argument.

8a Writing in a Style Appropriate for Your Field of Study

Each discipline has its own special language, style of expression, and manuscript format. You will, in time, learn fully the style for the field in which you major. Meanwhile, a few characteristics to guide your writing for papers in the humanities, social sciences, and sciences are identified in the following examples.

Academic Style in the Humanities

Writing in the humanities will require you to adopt a certain style, as shown in the following example written in CMS (Chicago).

> Organ and tissue donation is the gift of life. Each year many people confront health problems due to diseases or congenital birth defects. Tom Taddonia explains that tissues such as skin, veins, and valves can be used to correct congenital defects, blindness, visual impairment, trauma, burns, dental defects, arthritis, cancer, vascular and heart disease.[8] Steve Barnill says, "More than 400 people each month receive the gift of sight through yet another type of tissue donation—corneal transplants. In many cases, donors unsuitable for organ donation are eligible for tissue donation."[9] Barnill notes that tissues are now used in orthopedic surgery, cardiovascular surgery, plastic surgery, dentistry, and podiatry.[10] Even so, not enough people are willing to donate organs and tissues.

Writing in the humanities often displays these characteristics:

- Preoccupation with the quality of life, of art, of ideas (as shown in the first sentence of the example and as echoed in the final sentence).
- Personal involvement in ethical standards.

- Use of the present tense to indicate that this problem is an enduring one for humans of past ages as well as the present and the future.
- Use of CMS note style or MLA style for documenting the sources.
- Discussion of theory as supported by the literature.

Academic Style in the Social Sciences

A social science student might write the same passage in APA style:

> Organ and tissue donation has been identified as a social as well as a medical problem in North America. On one side, people have confronted serious problems in securing organs and tissue to correct health problems; on the other, people have demonstrated a reluctance to donate their organs. This need has been identified by Barnill (1999), Ruskin (2000), Taddonia (2001), and others. This hypothesis remains: People are reluctant to sign their donor cards. Consequently, this study will survey a random set of 1000 persons who have driver's licences to investigate the reasons for signing or not signing for donation. Further investigation can then be conducted to determine ways of increasing participation by potential donors.

Writing in the social sciences typically displays these characteristics:

- An objective approach to the topic.
- Fewer quotations from the sources, anticipating that readers will examine the literature for themselves.
- Use of past tense or the past participle in references to the source material.
- Use of APA style for documenting the sources.
- Discussion of theory as supported by the literature.
- Awareness that this research will prompt further study.

Academic Style in the Physical and Medical Sciences

A science student might write on this same topic in this way:

> Taddonia (1) has shown that human tissue can be used to correct many defects. Barnill (2) showed that more than 400 people receive corneal transplants each month. Yet the health profession needs more donors. It has been shown (3–6) that advanced care directives by patients with terminal illnesses would improve the donation of organs and tissue and relieve relatives of making any decision. Patients have been encouraged to complete organ donation cards (7) as well as to sign living wills (5, 8), special powers of attorney (5), and DNR (Do Not Resuscitate) Orders (5, 8). It is encouraged that advanced care directives become standard for the terminally ill.

Scientific or medical writing typically displays some of these characteristics:

- An objective approach to the topic without signs of personal commitment.

8a

- A search for a professional position (i.e., on organ donation).
- A preference for the passive voice and the past tense.
- Use of the CBE number system or, in some cases, the name and year system. (See Chapter 11, pages 138–40.)
- A reluctance to quote from the sources.
- A willingness to let a number represent the literature that will be cited with full documentation in the references section.

8b Focusing Your Argument

Your writing style in the research paper needs to be factual, but it should also reflect your thinking on the topic. Drafting the paper will happen more quickly if you focus on the central issues. Each paragraph will develop your primary claim.

Persuading, Inquiring, and Informing

Establishing a purpose for writing is one way to focus your argument. Do you wish to persuade or inquire and inform? *Persuasion* means that you wish to convince the reader that your position is valid and, perhaps, to ask the reader to take action. For example:

> Research has shown that homeowners and wild animals cannot live together in harmony. *Thus, we need to establish green zones in every city of this country to control the sprawl in urban areas and to protect a segment of the natural habitat for the animals.*

Inquiry is an exploratory approach to a problem in which you examine the issues and *inform* the reader of the results of the inquiry without the insistence of persuasion. You may need to examine, test, or observe in order to discuss the implications of the research. For example:

8b

> Many suburban home dwellers complain that deer, raccoons, and other wild animals ravage their gardens, flowerbeds, and garbage cans; however, the animals were there first. This study will examine the problem in one subdivision of 142 homes. How have animals been affected by the intrusion of human beings? How have homeowners been harassed by the animals? *The research will examine each side of the conflict by interviews with homeowners and observation of the animals.*

Note: In the above examples the thesis statement has been italicized.

Maintaining a Focus with Ethical and Logical Appeals

As an objective writer, you will need to examine the problem, make your claim, and provide supporting evidence. Moderation of your tone, even during argument, suggests control of the situation, both emotionally and intellectually. Your tone alerts the audience to your point of view in two ways:

1. **Ethical appeal.** If you project the image of one who knows and cares about the topic, the reader will recognize and respect your deep interest in the subject and the way you have carefully crafted your argument. The reader will also appreciate your attention to research conventions.
2. **Logical appeal.** For readers to believe in your position, you must provide sufficient evidence in the form of statistical data, paraphrases, and direct quotations from authorities on the subject.

The issue of organ donation, for example, elicits different reactions. Some people argue from the logical position that organs are available and should be used for those in need. Others argue from the ethical position that organs might be harvested prematurely or that organ donation violates religious principles. Some people are objective in their views; others are subjective. As a writer, you must balance your ethical and logical appeals to your readers.

Refining the Thesis Statement

A thesis is a statement or theory supported by arguments. Make sure your thesis statement satisfies all the following requirements:

1. Sets the argument to give focus to the entire paper.
2. Gives order to details of the essay by providing unity and a sense of direction.
3. Specifies to the reader the point of the research.

For example, Jennifer Kroetsch crafted this thesis:

> Consumers must consider the use of herbal remedies cautiously because of the possibility of dangerous side effects and the limited research on these products.

8b

This statement focuses the argument on the side effects of, and lack of research into, herbal remedies.

Using Questions to Focus the Thesis

If you have trouble focusing a thesis statement, ask yourself a few questions. In the previous example, Jennifer might have asked: What are the advantages of herbal remedies? How do they work? What are the serious side effects? What research on herbal remedies is available?

The next thesis developed from the question: "Do I have a new approach to guilt's impact on teen suicide?"

> THESIS   Recent research demonstrates that self-guilt often prompts a teenager to commit suicide.

The next thesis developed from the question: "What effect does poverty have on the crime statistics of juveniles?"

> THESIS   Personal economics is a force to be reckoned with; hence, poverty, not greed, forces many youngsters into a life of crime.

While questions may help develop the thesis, the thesis sentence makes a declarative statement that focuses the argument toward an investigative issue that will be resolved in the paper's discussion and conclusion.

Note: Even a "final" thesis may need adjustment as you develop the paper.

Using Key Words to Focus the Thesis

Use the important words from your notes and rough outline to refine your thesis statement. For example, during your reading of several novels by Margaret Laurence, you might have jotted down certain repetitions of image, theme, or character. The key words might be "liberation," "acceptance of self," "personal fulfillment," or other issues that Laurence explored time and again. These specific ideas might point you toward a general thesis:

> In her Manawaka novels, Margaret Laurence depicts women who break free from the roles imposed on them by their prairie small-town backgrounds.

Final Thesis Checklist

The thesis will fall short of expectations if it fails to answer "yes" to each of these questions:

1. Does it express your position in a full, declarative sentence that is not a question, not a statement of purpose, and not merely a topic?
2. Does it limit the subject to a narrow focus that grows out of research?
3. Does it establish an investigative, inventive edge to the interpretation or to the theoretical presentation?

8c

8c Designing an Academic Title

A clearly expressed title, developed early in the composing process, like a good thesis statement, will control your writing and keep you on course. Although writing a final title may not be feasible until the paper is written, the preliminary title can provide specific words of identification to help you stay focused. For example, one writer began with the title "Diabetes." Then the writer made it more specific: "Diabetes Management." As research developed and she recognized the role of medicine, diet, and exercise, she refined the title even more: "Diabetes Management: A Delicate Balance of Medicine, Diet, and Exercise." Thereby, she and her readers had a clear idea that the paper was about three methods of managing the disease.

Long titles are standard in scholarly writing. Your task is to give the reader a clear concept about the contents of the research paper, so use one of these strategies for writing your title:

1. Name a general subject, followed by a colon and a phrase that renames the subject ("Computer Control: Software Safeguards and Computer Theft").

2. Narrow a general subject with a prepositional phrase ("Religion in Public Schools").
3. Name a general subject and cite a specific work that will clarify the topic ("The Immigrant Experience in Brian Moore's *The Luck of Ginger Coffey*").
4. Name a general subject, followed by a colon, and followed by a phrase that describes the type of study ("Black Dialect in the Short Stories of Arna Bontemps: A Language Study").
5. Name a general subject, followed by a colon, and followed by a question ("Nuclear Energy: Do the Risks Outweigh the Benefits?").
6. Establish a specific comparison ("Women's Rights in Henrik Ibsen's *A Doll's House* and Alice Munro's *Lives of Girls and Women*").

Be sure to avoid fancy literary titles that may fail to label issues under discussion.

Poor	"Let There Be Hope"
Better	"Let There Be Hope: A View of Child Abuse"
Best	"Child Abuse: A View of the Victims"

For placement of the title, see one of these examples: MLA, page 112; APA, page 131; CBE, page 144; CMS, page 156.

8d Drafting the Paper

As you begin drafting your research paper, follow a few general guidelines:

8d

1. Work systematically through a preliminary plan or outline to keep order as your notes expand your research.
2. Leave wide margins, use triple spacing, and put blank spaces between paragraphs. Open areas in your writing will leave room for later revisions.
3. Use your notes, photocopies, downloaded material, and research journal to transfer materials directly into the text, either by hand or on your computer.
4. Provide quotations and paraphrases of key sentences, but avoid the temptation of borrowing too much.
5. Do not quote an entire paragraph unless it is crucial to your discussion and you cannot easily reduce it to a précis (see page 77).
6. Let the writing find its own way, guided, but not controlled, by your outline or paradigm.
7. Use different models and methods of development for different papers. See pages 37–40 for a detailed discussion of different models.
8. Do not expect a polished product at first. Initial drafts are exploratory and usually require additional reading, researching, and note taking.

These additional tips for drafting your paper may help:

Be practical. Begin by writing portions of the paper when you are ready, not only when you have a complete outline.

Be uninhibited. Initial drafts must be attempts to get words on the page rather than to create a polished document. Write without fear or delay.

Be judicious. Treat the sources with respect by citing names, enclosing quotations, and providing page numbers to the sources.

Drafting with a Computer

If you have developed your outline and notes on a computer, you can draft the paper from your outline and notes. You can do this in several ways:

1. Expand your outline to become the first draft of your research paper. Do this by importing your notes to a specific location of the outline and entering information underneath any of the outline headings as you develop ideas.
2. If you have placed all your notes within one file, begin writing your paper in a new file. As the writing progresses, find the note you wish to transfer, then CUT and COPY it. Go back to your text file and PASTE the note into your text.
3. In the file where you have placed all your notes, begin drafting the paper at the top of this file, which will push the notes below as you write. When you need a note, use FIND or SEARCH with the code word or title, then CUT and PASTE the note into your text.

Writing in the Proper Tense

Verb tense often distinguishes a paper in the humanities from one in the natural and social sciences. MLA style and CMS footnote style both require the present tense to cite an author's work (e.g., "Kozyrskyj *explains*" or "the work of Johnson and Stewart *shows*"). In contrast, APA style and CBE style both require the past tense or present perfect tense to cite an author's work (e.g., "Kozyrskyj *discovered*" or "the work of Johnson and Stewart *has demonstrated*"). When writing a paper in the humanities, use the historical present tense, as shown here in MLA style:

> Spear argues that Gentileschi's painting is clearly "a cathartic expression of the artist's private, and perhaps repressed, rage" (569).

Use the past tense in a humanities paper only for reporting historical events. In the next example, past tense is appropriate for all sentences *except* the last:

> In 1876, Alexander Graham Bell invented the telephone. Signals, sounds, and music had been sent by wire before, but Bell's instrument was the first to transmit speech. Bell's story, a lesson in courage and determination, is one worthy of study.

See Chapter 10, "Using APA Style" for additional discussion about using the correct tense in scientific style.

8d

Using the Language of the Discipline

Every discipline and every topic has its own vocabulary. Therefore, while reading and taking notes, jot down words and phrases relevant to the study. Get comfortable with the vocabulary of your topic so you can use it effectively. Nothing will betray a writer's ignorance of the subject more quickly than awkward and distorted technical terminology. For example, a child abuse topic requires the language of sociology, psychology, and medicine, thereby demanding an acquaintance with terms like:

aggressive behaviour	formative years	social worker
battered child	hostility	stress
behavioural patterns	maltreatment	trauma

Writing in the Third Person

Write your paper with an impersonal narration that avoids the use of the first person such as "I believe" or "It is my opinion." Rather than say, "I think objectivity on television is nothing more than an ideal," say, "Objectivity on television is nothing more than an ideal." Readers will understand that the statement is your thought.

Also avoid "we," "our," "you," and "your." Rather than say, "We must learn to be discriminating in our choice of television shows," use the third person and say, "Viewers must be discriminating in their choice of television shows."

Writing in the Passive Voice

Instructors often caution students against using the passive voice, which is often less forceful than using an active verb. However, research writers sometimes need to use the passive voice, as shown here:

> Forty-three students of a Grade 3 class at Barksdale School were observed for two weeks.

This usage of the passive voice is fairly standard in the social sciences and the natural or applied sciences. The passive voice is preferred because it keeps the focus on the subject of the research, not the writer.

Writing with Unity and Coherence

Unity gives writing a single vision; coherence connects the parts. Your paper has *unity* if it explores one topic in depth, with each paragraph carefully expanding upon a single aspect of the narrowed subject. A good organizational plan will help you achieve unity. Your paper has *coherence* if the parts are connected logically by

- repetition of key words and sentence structures
- the judicious use of pronouns and synonyms
- the effective placement of transitional words and phrases (e.g., *also, furthermore, therefore, in addition,* and *thus*)

The next passage moves with unity and coherence:

8d

Talk shows are spectacles of dramatic entertainment; therefore, members of the studio audience are acting out parts in the drama, like a Greek chorus, just as the host, the guest, and the television viewers are actors as well. Furthermore, some sort of interaction with the "characters" in this made-for-television "drama" happens all the time. While attending this "play," viewers analyze the presentation, determining for themselves what the drama means to them.

Note the use of the third person in the last sentence of the above passage.

Using Source Material to Enhance Your Writing

Readers want to discover *your* thoughts and ideas. For this reason, a paragraph should seldom contain source material only; it needs at the very least a topic sentence to establish a point for the research evidence. Every paragraph should explain, analyze, and support a thesis, not merely string together research information. Write with caution when working from photocopied pages of articles or books. You will be tempted to borrow too much. Quote or paraphrase key phrases and sentences; do not quote an entire paragraph unless it is crucial to your discussion and you cannot easily reduce it to a précis. The following passage, written in APA style, cites effectively two different sources.

Tabloid television is not so much news as entertainment. Pungente and O'Malley (1999) note: "The [long-running] *Today* show [. . .] gives viewers both information and entertainment, though sometimes the entertainment seems to take over, resulting in 'infotainment'" (p. 155). Another source notes that since "the networks live by the dictum 'keep it short and to the point,'" there is a concerted effort to make the news "lively" (Kuklinski and Sigelman, 2000, p. 821). Sadly, in some newscasts, viewer reaction seems to dictate the presentation of the facts.

8d

This passage illustrates four points. A writer must

- weave the sources effectively into a whole
- cite each source separately, one at a time
- provide different in-text citations
- use the sources as a natural extension of the discussion

Placing Graphics Effectively

Use graphics to support your text. Place graphics as close as possible to the parts of the text to which they relate. It is acceptable to use full-colour art if your printer will print in colours; however, use black for the captions and date. Place a full-page graphic design on a separate sheet after making a textual reference to it (e.g., "see Table 7"). Place graphic designs in an appendix when you have several complex items that might distract the reader from your textual message.

Avoiding Sexist and Biased Language

The best writers exercise caution against words that may stereotype any person, regardless of gender, race, nationality, creed, age, or disability. The following are some guidelines to help you avoid discriminatory language.

Age

Review the accuracy of your statement. It is appropriate to use *boy* and *girl* for children of high school age and under. *Young man* and *young woman* or *male adolescent* and *female adolescent* can be appropriate, but *teenager* carries a certain bias. Avoid *elderly* as a noun; use *older persons*.

Gender

Gender is a matter of our culture that identifies men and women within their social groups. *Sex* tends to be a biological factor. (See below for a discussion of sexual orientation.)

- Use plural subjects so that non-specific, plural pronouns are grammatically correct. For example, you may specify that Judy Jones maintains *her* lab equipment in sterile condition or indicate that technicians, in general, maintain *their* own equipment.
- Reword the sentence so that a pronoun is unnecessary, as in *The doctor prepared the necessary surgical equipment without interference.*
- Use pronouns that denote gender only when necessary when gender has been previously established, as in *Mary, as a new laboratory technician, must learn to maintain her equipment in sterile condition.*
- The use of *woman* and *female* as adjectives varies. Use *woman* or *women* in most instances (e.g., *a woman's intuition*) and use *female* for species and statistics, (e.g., *four female subjects*). Avoid the use of *lady,* as in *lady pilot.*
- In MLA and CMS styles the first mention of a person requires the full name (e.g., Charles Dickens or Carol Shields) and thereafter requires only the use of the surname (e.g., Dickens or Shields). In general, avoid formal titles (e.g., Dr., Gen., Mrs., Ms., Lt., Professor). Avoid their equivalents in other languages (e.g., Mme, Dame, Monsieur).
- Avoid unequal phrasing such as *man and wife* or *7 men and 16 females.* Keep the terms parallel by saying *husband and wife* or *man and woman* and *7 male rats and 16 female rats.*

8d

Sexual Orientation

The term *sexual orientation* is preferred to the term *sexual preference*. It is preferable to use *lesbians* and *gay men* rather than *homosexuals*. The terms *heterosexual, homosexual,* and *bisexual* can be used to describe both the identity and the behaviour of subjects.

Ethnic and Racial Identity

The preferred term in Canada is *Aboriginal*, rather than *Native*, because Aboriginal is a broader term that includes Status, Non-status, Inuit, and Métis persons. In historical contexts the terms *Native* and *Indian* are acceptable. The term *First Nations* should be used judiciously because it includes Status and Non-status Aboriginal persons but excludes Métis and Inuit persons. In the United States, *Native American* is a broad term that includes Samoans, Hawaiians, and American Indians.

Some persons prefer the term *Black,* others prefer *African American,* and still others prefer *a person of colour.* The terms *Negro* and *Afro-American* are now dated and not appropriate. Use *Black* and *White,* not the lowercase *black* and *white.* In like manner, some individuals may prefer *Hispanic, Latino, Mexican,* or *Chicano.* Use the term *Asian, Asian Canadian* or *Asian American* rather than *Oriental.* A good general rule is to use a person's nationality when it is known (*Mexican, Korean,* or *Nigerian*).

Disability

In general, place people first, not their disability. Rather than *a learning disabled person,* say *a person with a learning disability.* Instead of saying *a challenged person* or *a special child,* say *a person with a spinal cord injury* or *a child with Down syndrome.* Avoid making reference to a disability unless it is relevant to the discussion.

8e Creating an Introduction, Body, and Conclusion

Writing the Introduction

Use the first few paragraphs of your paper to establish the nature of your study. It should be long enough to establish the required elements described in the checklist below.

8e

Checklist for the Introduction

SUBJECT   Does your introduction identify your specific topic, and then define, limit, and narrow it to one issue?

BACKGROUND   Does your introduction provide relevant historical data or discuss a few key sources that touch on your specific issue?

PROBLEM   Does your introduction identify a problem and explain the complications that your research paper will explore or resolve?

THESIS STATEMENT   Does your introduction have a thesis statement that establishes the direction of the study and points your readers toward your eventual conclusions? Is your thesis statement placed at or near the end of the introduction?

How you work these essential elements into the framework of your opening will depend upon your style of writing. They need not appear in this order. Nor should you cram all these items into a short, opening paragraph. Feel free to write a longer introduction by using more than one of these techniques:

- Open with a quotation.
- Use an anecdote as a hook.
- Relate your topic to the well known.
- Provide background information.
- Review the literature briefly.
- Provide a brief summary.
- Define key terms.
- Supply data, statistics, and special evidence.
- Take exception to critical views.
- State the thesis (usually at the end of your one- or two-paragraph introduction).

The following sample of an introduction in MLA style gives background information, establishes a persuasive position, takes exception, gives key terms, and states the thesis in the last sentence.

8e

> Michel Tremblay's <u>Les Belles-Soeurs</u> premiered in Montreal in 1968. It is a funny, thought-provoking, controversial drama about 14 working-class women in east-end Montreal in the late 1960s who gather one evening to help their relative and neighbour, Germaine Lauzon, stick one million Gold Star stamps into booklets so she can redeem them for "valuable prizes." During this stamp-sticking party, the women vent their frustrations—about being poor, about being oppressed by men and the Church, about being women, and about being Québécoise. Tremblay's play has been acclaimed as "a classic" which "shocked and revolutionized Quebec Theatre" (Cottrell). Indeed, Tomson Highway has indicated that his award-winning portrayal of Aboriginal women in <u>The Rez Sisters</u> owes much to Tremblay's work. In spite of critical acclaim, however, the coarse language (*joual*) and daring themes in <u>Les Belles-Soeurs</u> stirred up much controversy in the late 1960s, and the successful revivals of the 1990s still shocked some audiences. Mixed reaction to <u>Les Belles-Soeurs</u> may well be because at the heart of this drama lies a disquieting theme: "the emotional turbulence of a people struggling to win a protected place in which they can develop in their own unique way" (Clarkson).

Avoiding Certain Mistakes in the Opening

Avoid a purpose statement, such as "The purpose of this study is . . ." unless your paper reports speculative research associated with the sciences. (See Chapter 10, "Using APA Style".)

Avoid repetition of the title, which should appear on the title page or first page of the text anyway.

Avoid a quotation that has no context; that is, you have not blended the quotation into the discussion clearly and effectively.

Avoid complex or difficult questions that may puzzle the reader; however, general rhetorical questions are acceptable.

Avoid simple dictionary definitions, such as *"The Canadian Oxford Dictionary* defines *monogamy* as the practice or state of being married to one person at a time."

Writing the Body

When writing the body of the paper, you should trace, classify, compare, and analyze the various issues. Keep in mind three elements, as shown in the checklist below.

Checklist for the Body of the Paper

ANALYSIS Classify the major issues of the study and provide a careful analysis of each in defence of your thesis.

PRESENTATION Provide well-reasoned statements at the beginning of your paragraphs and supply evidence of support with proper documentation.

PARAGRAPHS Vary development to compare, show process, narrate the subject's history, show causes, and so forth.

Use these techniques to build substantive paragraphs for your paper:

- Relate a time sequence.
- Compare or contrast issues, critics, and literary characters.
- Develop cause and effect.
- Issue a call to action.
- Define key terminology.
- Show a process.
- Ask questions and provide answers.
- Cite evidence from source materials.

The following paragraph in MLA style demonstrates the use of several techniques—establishing an overview of the problem, citing a source, comparing issues, showing cause and effect, noting key terms, and describing process.

To burn or not to burn the forests in the national parks is the question. The pyrophobic public voices its protests while environmentalists praise the rejuvenating effects of a good forest fire. It is difficult to convince people that not all fire is bad. The public has visions of Smokey the Bear campaigns and mental images of Bambi and Thumper fleeing the roaring flames. Perhaps the

8e

public could learn to see beauty in fresh green shoots, like Bambi and Faline as they returned to raise their young. Chris Bolgiano explains that federal policy evolved slowly "from the basic impulse to douse all fires immediately to a sophisticated decision matrix based on the functions of any given unit of land" (23). Bolgiano declares that "timber production, grazing, recreation, and wilderness preservation elicit different fire-management approaches" (23).

Writing the Conclusion

The conclusion is not a summary; it is a discussion of beliefs based on your reasoning and on the evidence that has been presented. Use the checklist below.

Checklist for the Conclusion

THESIS   Reaffirm the thesis statement and the central mission of your study. If appropriate, state your support for or criticism of an original hypothesis.

JUDGMENTS   Discuss and interpret the findings. Give answers. Now is the time to draw inferences, emphasize a theory, and find relevance in the details of the results.

DIRECTIVES   Based on the theoretical implications of the study, offer suggestions for action and new research.

8e

Use these techniques to write the conclusion:

- Restate the thesis and reach beyond it.
- Close with an effective quotation.
- Return the focus of a literary study to the author.
- Compare the past to the present.
- Offer a directive or a solution.
- Give a call to action.

Notice in the following example in MLA style how the writer begins the conclusion by restating the thesis and then uses other techniques to bring the essay's ideas to a conclusion:

Real or unreal, objectivity is something seldom, if ever, found on television. Ultimately, the media analyst must question why by 1998 both The Jerry Springer Show and The Oprah Winfrey Show were both averaging nearly seven million viewers a day (Pungente and O'Malley 158), and why the first morning talk show, Today, has lasted close to half a century. According to one critic, talk shows provide "instant, vivid, and easy to consume information about a wide and growing range of public affairs" (Kuklinski and Sigelman 810). As well, tabloid television gives people a way to feel good about themselves. Philip Marchand notes in <u>The Toronto Star</u> on January 4, 1997, that "(viewers) can watch these people and still feel . . . a valuable and attractive member of the human race." While watching the chronicles of the rich and famous or the struggles of people with bizarre problems, television viewers are helping to define their own subjective reality within the boundaries of the objective world and the symbolic reality of television.

Avoiding Certain Mistakes in the Conclusion

Avoid including afterthoughts or additional ideas; the conclusion is the place to end the paper, not begin new thoughts. If new ideas occur as you write your conclusion, don't ignore them. Explore them fully in the context of your thesis, and consider adding them to the body of your paper or slightly modifying your thesis. Scientific studies often discuss options and possible alterations that might affect test results.

Avoid the use of "thus," "in conclusion," or "finally" at the beginning of the last paragraph. Readers will be able to see that you are concluding the paper.

Avoid ending the paper without a sense of closure.

Avoid asking questions that raise new issues; however, writing rhetorical questions that restate the issues is acceptable.

8f Revising the Rough Draft

Revision can turn a passable paper into an excellent one and change an excellent paper into a brilliant research project. First, you should revise your paper on a global scale, moving blocks of material around to the best advantage and into the proper format. Second, revise your introduction, body and conclusion in more detail. Finally, edit the draft and proofread the final manuscript.

8f

Global Revision Checklist

1. Skim through the paper to check its unity. Does the paper maintain a central proposition from paragraph to paragraph?
2. Transplant paragraphs, moving them to more relevant and effective positions.
3. Delete sentences that do not further your cause.
4. Revise your outline to match these changes if you must submit the outline with the paper.

Revising the Introduction, Body, and Conclusion

Examine your **introduction** for the presence of several items:

1. Your thesis statement
2. A clear direction or plan of development
3. A sense of involvement that invites the reader into your investigation of a problem

Use the following as a guide for revising each paragraph in the **body** of your paper:

1. Cut out wordiness and irrelevant thoughts. Delete sentences that contribute nothing to the paper.
2. Combine any short paragraphs with others, or build a short paragraph into one of substance.
3. Revise long, difficult paragraphs by dividing them or by using transitions effectively. (See "Writing with Unity and Coherence," page 76.)
4. Omit paragraphs that seem short, shallow, or weak, or add more commentary and evidence to them, especially quotations from the primary source or critical citations from secondary sources.
5. Add your own input to paragraphs that rely too heavily on source materials.
6. Examine your paragraphs for transitions that move the reader effectively from one paragraph to the next.

Finally, examine the ending for a **conclusion** that (1) you have drawn from the evidence, (2) you have developed logically from the introduction and the body, and (3) has been determined by your position on the issues. (See also "Writing the Conclusion of the Paper," pages 82–83.)

8g Editing and Preparing the Final Manuscript

The cut-and-paste revision period is complemented by a session devoted to editing your sentences and your word choices. Use the following techniques to improve your final draft.

8h

1. Cut phrases and sentences that do not advance your main ideas or that merely repeat what your sources have already stated.
2. Determine that coordinated, balanced ideas are appropriately expressed and that minor ideas are properly subordinated.
3. Change most of your "to be" verbs (e.g., *is, are, was*) to stronger active verbs.
4. Maintain the present tense in most verbs in MLA and CMS style manuscripts and the past tense in APA and CBE style manuscripts.
5. Convert passive structures to active if appropriate.
6. Confirm that you have introduced paraphrases and quotations so they flow smoothly into your text.
7. Language should be elevated slightly in its formality, so avoid clusters of monosyllabic words that fail to advance ideas. Examine your wording for its effectiveness within the context of your subject.

8h Proofreading the Final Manuscript

After you have edited the text to your satisfaction, print a copy of the manuscript. Check for double spacing, one-inch margins, running heads with page numbers, and so forth. Even if you used available software to check your spelling, grammar, and style, you must nevertheless proofread this final version.

Note: Before and during the final printing of the manuscript, consult the Appendix, "Glossary of Manuscript Style," pages 163–176, which provides tips on handling the technicalities of margins, pagination, dates, numbers, and other matters.

Proofreading Checklist

1. Check for errors in sentence structure, spelling, and punctuation.
2. Check for hyphenation and word division. Remember that no words should be hyphenated at the ends of lines. If you are using a computer, turn off the automatic hyphenation.
3. Read each quotation for accuracy of your own wording and of the words within your quoted materials. Look, too, for your correct use of quotation marks.
4. Double check in-text citations to be certain that each one is correct and that each source is listed on your "Works Cited" (MLA and CMS) or "References" (APA and CBE) page at the end of the paper.
5. Double check the format: the title page, margins, spacing, and many other elements, as explained in Chapters 9 (MLA), 10 (APA), 11 (CBE), and 12 (CMS), and in the Appendix on pages 163–176.

8h

9 Using MLA Style

This chapter is devoted to the style set by the Modern Language Association (MLA), a group of professionals who set the standards for writing research papers on literature, English usage, foreign languages, and on occasion other subjects in the humanities. This chapter explains how to blend the source material into your writing, how to formulate and arrange the entries for your "Works Cited" listing (bibliography), and how to type and format various pages of the text. A sample paper in MLA style is provided on pages 112–117.

Consult the *MLA Handbook for Writers of Research Papers*, 5th edition, for more details of this style. Other styles are explained in Chapters 10 (APA), 11 (CBE), and 12 (CMS). Always check with your instructors as to which documentation style they prefer you to use. Also check whether titles of works should be italicized or underlined. (See Chapter 2, page 11 and the Appendix, page 172 for more information on italics and underlining.)

9a Blending Sources into Your Writing

The MLA style puts great emphasis upon the writer of your source, asking for the full name of the author on the first mention, but with only the last name thereafter. Use only the last name in parenthetical citations. Blend the sources into your writing with unity and coherence. Your sources will contribute **unity** to your paper because a quotation, a paraphrase, and a summary will explain and support your paragraph's topic sentence. A collection of random quotations, even though they deal with the same topic, is unacceptable. The source material contributes to **coherence** because introductions, transitions, and repetition of key words tie the paraphrase or the quotation to your exposition. (See also "Writing with Unity and Coherence," page 76.)

An *in-text citation*, sometimes called a *parenthetical reference*, is a reference that you blend into the text of your paper. Notice how the following example of in-text citation uses names and page numbers in two different ways. In the first sentence, the name of the authority introduces the quotation, with the page number after the quotation. In the second sentence, the writer's last name appears with the page number.

> According to Donna Smyth, Carol Shields' fictional world is "the middle ground of North American suburbia" (102). The reader's interest is sustained by "Shields' deft perceptions and crisp wit applied to the trivia of domestic life" (Moss 329).

Keep in-text citations brief. Remember that your readers will have full documentation to each source in the "Works Cited" list. (See page 94 for details on writing the "Works Cited" page.)

Making a General Reference without a Page Number

Sometimes you will need no parenthetical reference, as with

> Life on the Canadian prairies is the special focus of novels by Margaret Laurence, W. O. Mitchell, and Martha Ostenso.

Beginning with the Author and Ending with a Page Number

Introduce a quotation or a paraphrase with the author's name and close it with a page number, placed inside the parentheses:

> David Suzuki describes his experiences in Japan where he was treated as a "gaijin" or foreigner (300).

Putting the Page Number Immediately after the Name

Sometimes, notes at the end of a quotation make it expeditious to place the page number after the name of the source.

> Kozyrskyj (698) notes that "one in five Canadians have used some form of <u>alternative</u> therapy such as . . . herbalism" (emphasis added).

Putting the Name and Page Number at the End of Borrowed Material

As an alternative, you may put cited names with the page number within parentheses.

> "This shift in the role of art and artist is a difficult one for Ondaatje to make, for it means surrendering the dream of originality" (Ferris 78).

Citing a Source When No Author Is Listed

When no author is shown on a title page, cite the title of an article, the name of the magazine, the name of a bulletin or book, or the name of the publishing organization:

> Newfoundland is the oldest place name of European origin in Canada [. . .] [with] places named Pushthrough, Cutthroat, Seldom Come By, Blow Me Down, Come-by-Chance, Boxey, or Bumble Bee Bight. The latter are a few of the toponymic delights of Newfoundland and Labrador (<u>Teaching and Learning about Canada</u> 55).

Identifying Non-Printed Sources

On occasion you may need to identify non-printed sources, such as a speech, the song lyrics from a compact disc, an interview, or a television program. Since there is no page number, omit the parenthetical citation. Instead, introduce the type of source (i.e., lecture, letter, or interview) so readers do not expect a page number.

9a

Rudyk's lecture emphasized that "plagiarism is a serious academic offence which can result in dire consequences."

Identifying Internet Sources

Currently, most Internet sources have no prescribed page numbers or numbered paragraphs. You cannot list the screen numbers or the page numbers of a downloaded document because computer screens and printers differ. Therefore, provide a paragraph number or a page number *only* if the author of the Internet article has provided it. The marvellous feature of electronic text is that it is searchable, so your readers can find your quotation quickly with the browser's FIND feature. Suppose that you have written the following:

> In 1992, the Canadian Radio-television and Telecommunications Commission (CRTC) established the long-term goal of making violence on television "socially unacceptable, in much the same way as has already been done in Canada with other social issues such as drinking and driving, pollution, and cigarette smoking" (<u>CRTC Factsheet: Canada and TV Violence: Cooperation and Consensus</u> 1996).

A reader who wants to investigate further will find your complete citation on your "Works Cited" page. There the reader will discover the Internet address for the article. Try to identify the author of an Internet article if possible.

> Susan Merritt discusses the fight of the "Famous Five" to have women legally recognized as persons in Canada.

If you cannot identify an author, give the article title or website information.

> In 1920 Dr. Frederick Banting had an idea that would "unlock the mystery of the dreaded diabetes disorder" ("The Discovery of Insulin: A Canadian Medical Miracle of the 20th Century").

9a

Establishing the Credibility of the Source

In some instances, your instructors may expect you to indicate your best estimate of a source's scholarly value. For example, the following citation might be introduced in this way to verify the validity of the source:

> Allon Reddoch, president of the Canadian Medical Association (CMA), states that opening the Office of Natural Health Products is "a first step" in recognizing that urgent regulatory action is needed "to maximize the benefits of natural health products while minimizing their risks" (Sibbald).

To learn more about the source of an Internet article, as in the case immediately above, learn to search out a home page. Reddoch's comment is from an article in the *Canadian Medical Association Journal*. The address for this article is **www.cma.ca/cmaj/vol-160/issue-9/1355.htm**. By truncating the address to **www.cma.ca**, you can learn more about the Canadian Medical Association, and to find other articles in the journal you can consult **www.cma.ca/cmaj**. See also "Evaluating Internet Sources," in 3d, page 29.

Citing Indirect Sources

Sometimes the writer of a book or article will quote another person from an interview or personal correspondence, and you will want to use that same quotation. Conform to this next example, which cites the person making the statement (Greenburg) and then cites the source where you found the material (Peterson).

> After students get beyond middle school, they begin to resent interference by their parents, especially in school activities. They need some space from Mom and Dad. Martin Greenburg says, "The interventions can be construed by the adolescent as negative, overburdening and interfering with the child's ability to care for himself" (qtd. in Peterson 9).

Without the reference to Greenburg, it would be difficult to find the article, and readers would assume that Peterson had spoken the words.

Citing Frequent Page References of a Work

When you make frequent references to the same source, you need not repeat the author's name in every instance; a specific page reference is adequate, or you can provide act, scene, and line if appropriate. Note the following example:

> Each of the characters in Highway's <u>The Rez Sisters</u> has her own reason for wanting to win The Biggest Bingo in the World. Veronique yearns for "a great big stove, the kind Madame Benoit has" (36), Annie "will go to every record store in Toronto . . . and buy the biggest (record player) in the world" (35), and Philomena wants to find the child she gave up 28 years ago (81). The most poignant yearning of all, however, is that of Maria-Adele, who has been diagnosed with cancer: "I'm gonna buy me an island . . . the most beautiful island in the world" (36).

Citing from Two or More Novels

If you are citing from two or more novels in your paper, let's say Margaret Atwood's <u>The Edible Woman</u> and <u>The Handmaid's Tale</u>, provide both the title, abbreviated, and the page(s) unless the reference is clear: (<u>Edible</u> 15) and (<u>Handmaid's</u> 24–25).

Citing Material from Textbooks and Anthologies

If you quote a passage from a textbook or anthology, and if that is all you quote from the anthology, cite the author and page in the text and put a comprehensive entry in the "Works Cited" list. In the text write:

> In "The Skaters" John Gould Fletcher compares "the grinding click" of ice skates to "the brushing together of thin wing-tips of silver" (814).

In the bibliography ("Works Cited"), write:

> Fletcher, John Gould. "The Skaters." <u>Patterns in Literature</u>. Ed. Edmund J. Farrell, Ouida H. Clapp, and Karen Kuehner. Glenview: Scott, 1991. 814.

9a

See page 97 for another example of a bibliography entry for individual works within an anthology.

Adding Extra Information to In-Text Citations

As a courtesy to your reader, add extra information within the citation. Show parts of books, different titles by the same writer, or several works by different writers. For example, your reader may have a different anthology than yours, so a clear reference such as "The Great Santini 294; chap. 21," will enable the reader to locate the passage. Moreover, with a reference to "Much Ado about Nothing 2.1.42–43," the reader will find the passage in any edition of Shakespeare's play.

Cite several authors in one citation, as shown next:

> Several sources have addressed this aspect of gang warfare as a
> fight for survival, not just for control of the local turf (Rollins 34;
> Templass 561–65; Robertson 98–134).

There is no required listing order in MLA style (APA requires listing in alphabetical order by the authors' surnames). Note, however, that multiple citations are not encouraged in MLA style since they may be confusing to the reader.

9b Punctuating Citations Correctly and Consistently

Keep parenthetical citations outside quotation marks but inside the final period, as shown here:

> Slatkin notes that Artemisi Gentileschi "expressed her identity as a
> woman and as an artist" (54).

The exception occurs with long indented quotations, which do not use quotation marks at all (see page 91).

Commas and Periods

Place commas and periods inside quotation marks unless the page citation intervenes. The example below shows (1) how to put the mark inside the quotation marks, (2) how to interrupt a quotation to insert the speaker, (3) how to use single quotation marks within the regular quotation marks, and (4) how to place the period after a page citation.

> "Modern advertising," says Rachel Murphy, "not only creates a
> marketplace, it determines values." She adds, "I resist the
> advertiser's argument that they 'awaken, not create desires'" (192).

Semicolons and Colons

Both semicolons and colons go outside the quotation marks, as illustrated by this example:

> Pierre Berton comments, "After centuries we've cut our last ties with
> Europe and we're officially independent" (283); nevertheless, as
> Berton observes, we still have a Queen.

Question Marks and Exclamation Marks

When a question mark or an exclamation mark serves as part of a quotation, keep it inside the quotation mark. Put the page citation immediately after the name of the source, as shown below.

> Judy LaMarsh (225) states that one of the first questions she was asked after being elected to Parliament was, "Are you a politician, or a woman?"

Quotation Marks

Single Quotation Marks

When a quotation is enclosed within another quotation, use single quotation marks around the enclosed quotation.

> George Loffler confirms that "the unconscious carries the best of human thought and gives man great dignity, but it also has the dark side so that we cry, in the words of Shakespeare's Macbeth, 'Hence, horrible shadow! Unreal mockery, hence'" (32).

Long Quotations

Set off long prose quotations of four lines or more by indenting one inch, two clicks of the tab key, or 10 spaces. Do not use quotation marks with the indented material. If you quote only one paragraph or the beginning of one, do not indent an extra five spaces. Maintain the same spacing between your text and the quoted materials. Place the parenthetical citation *after* the final mark of punctuation, as shown below:

> In discussing the traits of successful television news anchors, two Canadian media analysts make this observation:
>
> > Worth noting, too, [is] how acceptable Canadians seem to be on American television as anchors. ABC employees joke that their call letters stand for "America By Canadians." The two best known are Peter Jennings at ABC and Morley Safer, who has co-hosted CBS's <u>60 Minutes</u> for nearly 30 years. (Pungente and O'Malley 189)
>
> Pungente and O'Malley go on to discuss the reasons for the appeal of Canadian news anchors south of the border.

9b

Quotations from Poetry

Incorporate short quotations of poetry (one or two lines) into your text. Use a slash to show line breaks.

> Part 3 of Eliot's "The Waste Land" (1922) remains a springtime search for nourishing water: "Sweet Thames, run softly, for I speak not loud or long" (3.12) says the speaker in "The Fire Sermon," while in Part 5 the speaker of "What the Thunder Said" yearns for "a damp gust / Bringing rain" (5.73–74).

Quotations from Drama

Set off from your text any dialogue of two or more characters. Begin with the character's name, indented one inch from the left margin and written in all capital letters. Follow the name with a period.

> At the end of <u>Oedipus Rex</u>, Kreon chastises Oedipus, reminding him that he no longer has control over his own life nor that of his children.
>
> > KREON.   Come now and leave your children.
> > OEDIPUS.   No! Do not take them from me!
> > KREON.   Think no longer
> > > That you are in command here, but
> >
> > rather think
> > > How, when you were, you served
> >
> > your own destruction.

Refer to act, scene, and lines only after you have established the author and title of the work under discussion. For example, indicate that Shakespeare's <u>Henry IV, Part 1</u> is the central topic of your study; thereafter, use a shortened reference, such as "(<u>1H4</u> 1.1.15–18)."

Initial Capitals in Quoted Matter

In general, you should reproduce quoted materials exactly; however, one exception is permitted for logical reasons. Restrictive connectors, such as *that* or *because,* create restrictive clauses and eliminate a need for the comma. Without a comma, the capital letter is unnecessary. In the following example, "The," which is capitalized as the first word in the original sentence, is changed to lower case and enclosed in brackets because it continues the grammatical flow of the student's sentence.

> In his text <u>More Canada Firsts</u>, Conacher notes that "[the] Montreal Canadiens have won more championships, division titles and playoff games than any other professional sports team in the world" (172).

9b

Ellipsis Points for Omitted Material

You may omit portions of quoted material and signal the omission with three spaced ellipsis points set within brackets. In omitting material, do not change the meaning or take a quotation out of context.

Omitting Material within a Sentence

Use three *spaced* ellipsis points (periods) in brackets to signal material omitted within a sentence:

> Peter Gzowski comments, "Hockey was the common Canadian coin [. . .] the men—and sometimes the women who followed it came from every class and every region" (279).

Omitting Material at the End of a Sentence

If an ellipsis occurs at the end of your sentence, use spaced ellipsis points within brackets and follow the closing bracket with the sentence period and the closing quotation mark.

Desmond Morton (xv) declares that "most Canadians, French- and English-speaking, First Nations and newcomers, take a quiet pride in this country [. . .]."

If a page citation also appears at the end, use three spaced ellipsis points within brackets, close the quotation, add the page citation, and then add the period.

Desmond Morton declares that "most Canadians, French- and English-speaking, First Nations and newcomers, take a quiet pride in this country [. . .]" (xv).

Omitting Complete Sentences and Paragraphs

When you omit an entire sentence or more, even a complete paragraph or more, end the sentence by using a period. Then, insert three spaced ellipsis points in brackets.

Conacher reminds us that "Alex Trebek, a Canadian from Sudbury, Ontario, has reached the pinnacle of game shows, hosting the very popular TV show <u>Jeopardy</u> since 1984. [. . .] He has appeared in over thirty TV shows and films, and his role has almost always been as the host of <u>Jeopardy</u>" (120).

Omitting Material in Lines of Poetry

If you omit a word or phrase in your quotation of poetry, indicate the omission with three or four ellipsis points just as you would with omissions in a prose passage. However, if you omit a complete line or more from the poem, indicate the omission by a line of bracketed spaced periods that equals the average length of the lines.

> Do ye hear the children weeping, O my brothers,
>> Ere the sorrow comes with years?
> They are leaning their young heads against their mothers,
>> And <u>that</u> cannot stop their tears.
> [. . . . .]
> They are weeping in the playtime of the others,
>> In the country of the free. (Browning 382)

Adding Explanations or Emphasis to a Quotation

You will sometimes need to alter a quotation to emphasize a point or to make something clear. You might add material, italicize an important word, or use the word *sic* (Latin for *thus* or *so*) to alert readers that you have properly reproduced the material even though the logic or the spelling of the original might appear to be in error. Use parentheses or brackets according to these basic rules:

Comment That Follows the Quotation

Use *parentheses* to enclose comments or explanations that immediately follow a quotation as shown in this example:

Kozyrskyj (698) notes that "one in five Canadians use some form of <u>alternative</u> therapy such as [. . .] herbalism" (emphasis added).

Comment inside the Quotation

Use *brackets* for **interpolation**, which means to insert new matter into a text or quotation. The use of brackets signals the insertion. Note the following examples:

Appositive (renames a word)

> This critic claims, "More intensely dramatic than <u>The Stone Angel</u>, this novel [<u>A Jest of God</u>] attempts somewhat less than its predecessor in both narrative technique and character development" (Moss 216).

Insertion of a Word

> "John F. Kennedy [was] an immortal figure of courage and dignity in the hearts of most Americans," notes one historian (Jones 82).

Personal Comment

> He says, for instance, that the "extended family is now rare in contemporary society, and with its demise the new parent has <u>lost the wisdom</u> [my emphasis] and daily support of older, more experienced family members" (Zigler 42).

Use of sic to Note an Error in the Original

> Sullivan says that during the October Crisis of 1970, "when Pierre Laporte, a federal minister [sic], was kidnapped and killed," the poet Gwendolyn MacEwan expressed her dread to Margaret Atwood (268).

Use the following checklist to guide your handling of the source material.

9c

Checklist for Blending Sources into the Text

1. Check that you have truly blended the sources into *your* writing.
2. Check that you have introduced and documented the sources correctly.
3. Check that you have indented quotations of four lines or more.

9c Writing the Works Cited Page in MLA Style

After writing your paper, prepare a "Works Cited" page to list your reference materials. List only the sources that you actually used in your manuscript. If you developed your working bibliography while developing your paper, the list of sources, arranged alphabetically, can provide the necessary information.

Select a heading that indicates the nature of your list.

1. Label the page with the heading "Works Cited" if your list includes only the printed works quoted and paraphrased in the paper.

2. Use the label *Sources Cited* if your list includes non-print items, such as an interview, speech, or Internet sources, as well as printed works.
3. Reserve the heading *Bibliography* for a complete listing of *all* works related to the subject, an unlikely prospect for undergraduate papers.

Arrange items in alphabetical order by the surname of the author using the letter-by-letter system. Consider the first names only when two or more surnames are identical. When two or more entries cite co-authors that begin with the same name, alphabetize by the last names of the second authors:

Harris, Walter, and David Bleich
Harris, Walter, and Stephen M. Fishman

When no author is listed, alphabetize by the first important word of the title. Set the title "Works Cited" or "Sources Cited" one inch down from the top of the sheet and double space between it and the first entry. See the sample "Sources Cited" in 6f on page 55 and "Works Cited" in 9e on page 117.

Bibliography Form—Books

Enter information for books in the following order. Items 1, 3, and 8 are required; add other items according to the rules that follow:

1. **Author(s)**
2. Chapter or part of the book
3. **Title of the book**
4. Editor, translator, or compiler
5. Edition
6. Volume number of the book
7. Name of the series
8. **Place, publisher, and date**
9. Page numbers
10. Total number of volumes

9c

Author

> Garrett-Petts, William F. Writing about Literature: A Guide for the Student Critic. Peterborough, ON: Broadview Press, 2000.

Author, Anonymous

> The Song of Roland. Trans. Frederick B. Luquines. New York: Macmillan, 1960.

Author, More Than One Work by the Same Author

Instead of repeating the author's name, use three hyphens followed by a period. List the works alphabetically by the title (ignoring *a, an,* and *the*).

> Rowling, J. K. Harry Potter and the Chamber of Secrets. New York: Scholastic, 1999.
> - - -. Harry Potter and the Goblet of Fire. New York: Scholastic, 2000.

- - -. Harry Potter and the Sorcerer's Stone. New York: Scholastic, 1998.

Authors, Two or Three

Diamond, Rick, and Candace Schaefer. The Creative Writing Guide: Poetry, Literary Nonfiction, Fiction and Drama. New York: Longman, 1998.

Authors, More Than Three

Use "et al.," which means "and others," or list all the authors.

Prentice, Alison, et al. *Canadian Women: A History*. 2nd ed. Toronto: Harcourt Brace Canada, 1996.

Author, Corporation, or Institution

A corporate author can be an association, a committee, or any group or institution when the title page does not identify the names of the members. List a committee or council as the author even when the organization is also the publisher, as in this example:

Canadian Council on Social Development. The Progress of Canada's Children 1999/2000. Ottawa: CSSD, 2000.

Alphabetized Works, Encyclopedias, and Biographical Dictionaries

Well-known works need only the edition and the year of publication:

Corelli, Rae. "How Are Canadians Different from Americans?" The Canadian Encyclopedia. World ed. 1999.

If no author is listed, begin with the title of the article:

"Kiosk: Word History." The American Heritage Dictionary of the English Language. 3rd ed. 1992.

Less-familiar reference works need a full citation, including publication information.

"Cortisone." Guide to Prescription and Over-the-Counter Drugs. New York: Random House, 1988.

The Bible

Do not underline or italicize the word "Bible" or the books of the Bible. Common editions need no publication information. Do underscore or italicize special editions of the Bible.

The Bible. Revised Standard Version.
The New Open Bible. Large print ed. Nashville: Thomas Nelson, 1990.

Classical Works

Homer. The Iliad. Trans. Richmond Lattimore. Chicago: U of Chicago P, 1951.

9c

Component Part of an Anthology or Collection

Provide the inclusive page numbers for the piece, not just the page or pages that you have cited in the text. Use this form:

> Came, Barry. "The Red River Flood, Spring, 1997." <u>In the Face of Disaster: True Stories of Canadian Heroism from the Archives of Maclean's</u>. Ed. Michael Benedict. Toronto: Viking, 2000. 68–75.

Cross References to Works in an Anthology or Collection

Cite several different selections from one anthology giving a full reference to the anthology and abbreviated cross references to the individual selections.

> Morton, Desmond, and Morton Weinfeld. <u>Who Speaks for Canada? Words That Shape a Country</u>. Toronto: McClelland & Stewart, 1998.
> Harper, Elijah. "No Ordinary Hero." Morton and Weinfeld 320–24.
> Mackenzie, Lewis. "Goodbye to Sarajevo". Morton and Weinfeld 317–320.
> Secord, Laura. "With Forced Courage." Morton and Weinfeld 8–9.

Edition

Cite any edition beyond the first.

> Buckley, Joanne. <u>Fit to Print: The Canadian Student's Guide to Essay Writing</u>. 5th ed. Toronto: Harcourt Canada, 2001.

Editor

List the editor first if your in-text citation refers to the work of the editor, (e.g., the editor's introduction or notes), as in "Bevington 316."

> Bevington, David, ed. <u>The Complete Works of Shakespeare</u>. 4th ed. New York: Harper, 1992.

9c

Encyclopedia

See "Alphabetized Works," page 96.

Manuscript Collections in Book Form

> <u>Cotton Vitellius</u>. A.XV. British Museum, London.
> Chaucer, Geoffrey. <u>The Canterbury Tales</u>. Harley ms. 7334. British Museum, London.

Play, Book Length

> Ryga, George. <u>The Ecstasy of Rita Joe</u>. Vancouver: Talonbooks, 1970.

Play, in an Anthology or Collection

> Shakespeare, William. <u>Macbeth</u>. <u>Shakespeare: Twenty-Three Plays and the Sonnets</u>. Ed. T. M. Parrott. New York: Scribner's, 1953.

Poem, Book Length

> Dante. <u>The Divine Comedy</u>. Trans. Lawrence G. White. New York:
> Pantheon, 1948.

Use this next form if you cite specific pages from a book-length poem:

> Eliot, T. S. <u>Four Quartets</u>. <u>The Complete Poems and Plays</u>
> <u>1909–1950</u>. New York: Harcourt, 1952. 115–45.

Poem, in an Anthology or Collection

Use this form with inclusive page numbers if you cite one poem from a collection:

> Eliot, T. S. "The Love Song of J. Alfred Prufrock." <u>The Complete</u>
> <u>Poems and Plays 1909–1950</u>. New York: Harcourt, 1952. 3–7.

Sourcebooks and Casebooks

> Ellmann, Richard. "Reality." <u>Yeats: A Collection of Critical Essays</u>.
> Ed. John Unterecker. Twentieth Century Views. Englewood
> Cliffs: Prentice, 1963. 163–74.

Title of a Book in Another Language

Use lower case letters for foreign titles except for the first word and proper names. Provide a translation in brackets if you think it necessary (e.g., <u>L'étranger</u> [<u>The Stranger</u>]). (For German titles, see "Foreign Languages," in the "Appendix", on page 174.)

> Brombert, Victor. <u>Stendhal et la voie oblique</u>. New Haven: Yale UP,
> 1954.

Volumes

> Dryden, John. <u>Poems 1649–1680. The Works of John Dryden</u>. Ed.
> Edward Niles Hooker et al. Vol. 1. Berkeley: U of California P,
> 1956.

9c

Bibliography Form—Periodicals

For journal or magazine articles, use the following order. Items 1, 2, 3, 7, and 8 are required.

1. **Author(s)**
2. **Title of the article**
3. **Name of the periodical**
4. Series number (if it is relevant)
5. Volume number (for journals)
6. Issue number (if needed)
7. **Date of publication**
8. **Page numbers**

Author

> Emilsson, Wilhelm. "Icelandic Voices." <u>Canadian Literature</u> 162
> (1999): 231–34.

Authors, Two or Three

Tate, Eugene D., Andrew Osler, and Gregory Fouts. "The Beginnings of Communication Studies in Canada: Remembering and Narrating the Past." <u>Canadian Journal of Communication</u> 25.1 (2000).

For more than three authors use "et al." or list all the authors, as for a book (see page 96).

Author, Anonymous

"Performance 2000." <u>Canadian Business</u> 25 June 1999: 62–128.

Interview, Published

Lowe, Rob. Interview. <u>Architectural Digest</u>. July 2001: 79+.

Journal with All Issues for a Year Paged Continuously

Barnett, Pamela E. "Figurations of Rape and the Supernatural in <u>Beloved</u>." <u>PMLA</u> 112 (1997): 418–27.

Journal with Each Issue Paged Anew

Add the issue number and/or the month after the volume number.

Suhor, Charles. "Censorship—When Things Get Hazy." <u>English Journal</u> 86.2 (Feb. 1997): 26–28.

Magazine, Monthly

Pigott, Paul. "Nunavut's Flag-Raising." <u>Canadian Geographic</u> Nov. 1997: 20.

Magazine, Weekly

Bemrose, John. "Al Waxman: Remembering the 'King.'" <u>Maclean's</u> 29 Jan. 2001: 59.

9c

Notes, Editorials, Queries, Reports, Comments, Letters

Ferreira-Buckley, Linda. "Comment and Response." <u>College English</u> 62 (2000): 524–37.
"Lost Treasure." Letter. <u>Library Journal</u> 2 July 2001: 3.

Reprint of a Journal Article

If the article is reprinted by an information service that gathers together several articles on a common topic, use the form shown in the following example.

Cox, Rachel S. "Protecting the National Parks." <u>The Environment</u>. <u>CQ Researcher</u> 16 July 2000: 523+. Washington, DC: Congressional Quarterly, 2000. No. 23.

If the service reprints articles from other sources, use this next form, which shows original publication data and then information on the *SIRS* booklet—title, editor, and volume number.

Hodge, Paul. "The Andromeda Galaxy." <u>Mercury</u> July/Aug. 1993: 98+. <u>Physical Science</u>. Ed. Eleanor Goldstein. Vol. 2. Boca Raton: SIRS, 1994. Art. 24.

Review Article

Tweedie, Katherine, and Michael Torosian. Rev. of <u>Michael Lambeth: Photographer</u>. <u>Journal of Canadian Art History</u> 10.2: 165–67.

Title within the Article's Title

Dundes, Alan. "'To Love My Father All': A Psychoanalytic Study of the Folktale Source of <u>King Lear</u>." <u>Southern Folklore Quarterly</u> 40 (1976): 353–66.

Title, Foreign

Rebois, Charles. "Les effets du 12 juin." <u>Le Figaro Magazine</u> 2 juillet 1994: 42–43.

Stivale, Charles J. "Le vraisemblable temporel dans <u>Le rouge et le noir</u>." <u>Stendhal Club</u> 84 (1979): 299–313.

Bibliography Form—Newspapers

Provide the name of the author; the title of the article; the name of the newspaper as it appears on the masthead, omitting any introductory article (e.g., <u>Globe and Mail</u>, not <u>The Globe and Mail</u>); and the complete date—day, month (abbreviated), and year. Omit any volume and issue numbers. Provide a page number as listed (e.g., 21, B–6, 14C, D3).

Newspaper in One Section

Wood-Mead, Marianne. "Euthanasia Bill Open to Abuse." <u>Winnipeg Sun</u> 17 Apr. 2001: 9

Newspaper with Lettered Sections

Powell, Betsy. "Richler's Greatest Work Was Husband, Father." <u>Toronto Star</u> 6 July 2001: A3.

Newspaper with Numbered Sections

Jones, Tim. "New Media May Excite, While Old Media Attract." <u>Chicago Tribune</u> 28 July 1997, sec. 4: 2.

Newspaper Column or Editorial with No Author Listed, City Added

"Legislative Endorsement." Editorial. <u>Tennessean</u> [Nashville] 31 July 2000: 12A.

Bibliography Form—Government Documents

The nature of public documents varies. Therefore, whether citing a print or electronic source, always provide as much information as you can to help the reader locate the exact source cited. Use the following guidelines for provincial and federal documents. Useful websites are the *Brief Guide to Citing*

9c

Canadian Government Documents **http://library.queensu.ca/webdoc/ guides/cancite.htm** and *Citing Canadian Government Documents* **www. info.library.yorku.ca/depts/bg/citing_can_govdocs.htm**. As well, consult the latest edition of the *MLA Handbook for Writers of Research Papers.*

The basic guidelines for citing government documents and publications in alternative styles such as APA (Chapter 10), CBE (Chapter 11) and CMS (Chapter 12) are similar, but make sure that citations for any government publications are consistent with the style used for other sources in your paper.

As a general rule, place information in the bibliographic entry in this order:

1. Government
2. Body or agency
3. Subsidiary body
4. Title of document
5. Identifying numbers
6. Publication facts

When you cite two or more works by the same government, substitute three hyphens for the name of each government or body that you repeat:

> Canada. Parliament. House of Commons.
> – – –. – – –. Senate.
> – – –. Dept. of Justice.

Government Departments and Agencies

If the name of the author of the document is known, cite the government document as follows:

> Baeyer, C. V. The Ancestry of Canadian English. Hull, PQ: Public
> Service Commission of Canada, 1980.

However, for either print or electronic citations, if no author is named, treat the government agency as the author. Give the name of the political jurisdiction (country, province, or municipality), followed by the name of the government body issuing the document, the title, edition, and publishing details:

> Canada. Supreme Court of Canada. The Supreme Court of Canada
> and Its Justices: 1875–2000. Ottawa: Dundurn Press, 2000.
> Prince Edward Island. Fishing, Aquaculture and Environment.
> Hunting Summary 2001. Charlottetown, PE: FAE, 2001.

If, as in the following example, the name of the government body begins with the same word, e.g., Canada or Canadian, you need not include the name of the jurisdiction.

> Canadian Mortgage and Housing Corporation. The Newcomer's
> Guide to Canadian Housing. Ottawa: CMHC, 1999.

Parliamentary and Legislative Documents

> Canada. Parliament. Senate. Journals of the Senate. 36th Parl. 2nd
> sess. No. 84 (20 Oct. 2000). Ottawa: Queen's Printer, 2000.

9c

Reports of Commissions and Standing Committees

Canada. Royal Commission on Aboriginal Peoples. <u>People to People,</u>
<u>Nation to Nation: Highlights from the Report of the Royal</u>
<u>Commission on Aboriginal Peoples</u>. Ottawa: The Commission,
1996.

Canada. Parliament. House of Commons. Standing Committee on
Human Resources Development and the Status of Persons
with Disabilities. <u>Beyond Bill C-2: Review of Other Proposals</u>
<u>to Reform Employment Insurance: Report of the Standing</u>
<u>Committee on Human Resources Development and the Status</u>
<u>of Persons with Disabilities</u>. Ottawa: The Committee, 2001.

Statutes

Only the short title of acts need be cited. Be sure to note the reading of bills.

Canada. <u>Youth Criminal Justice Act</u>, Bill C-3, First Reading, 14 Oct.
1999 (36th Parl., 2nd sess.).

When citing government documents on electronic sources, include the same
information as for printed sources, but be sure to include the government
agency or author who created the website, the date posted, the date
retrieved, and the website address (URL). See page 103 for examples and also
the *MLA Handbook*'s section 4.9.

Consult *The Complete Guide to Citing Government Information Resources:*
A Manual for Writers and Librarians, Rev. ed., 1993, by Diane Garner and
Diane Smith for more details on the correct bibliographic form for government
documents and publications.

Bibliography Form—Electronic Sources

For material that you use from the Internet, include these items as appropriate to the source:

1. Author/editor name, followed by a period
2. Title of an article in quotation marks, or the title of a posting to a discussion list or forum, followed by the words *online posting,* followed
   by a period
3. Name of the book, journal, or complete work, underlined or italicized
4. Publication information, followed by a period
   Place, publisher, and date for books
   Volume and year of a journal
   Exact date of a magazine
   Date and description for government documents
5. Name of the institution or organization sponsoring the website, if available
6. Date of your access, not followed by a comma or a period
7. Uniform Resource Locator (URL), within angle brackets, followed by a
   period. At the end of a line, break the URL only after a virgule (/), commonly termed a slash, or after a period, commonly termed a dot.

Note: Do not include page numbers unless the Internet article shows original page numbers from the printed version of the journal or magazine. Do not include the total number of paragraphs nor specific paragraph numbers unless the original Internet article has provided them.

Abstract of a Journal Article

Kilbourn, Russell, "Re-Writing 'Reality': Reading <u>The Matrix</u>." <u>Canadian Journal of Film Studies</u> 9 (2000). Abstract. 5 July 2001 <www.film.queensu.ca/FSAC/CJFS.html>.

Article from a Scholarly Journal

Clare, Janet. "Transgressing Boundaries: Women's Writing in the Renaissance and Reformation." <u>Renaissance Forum</u> 1. (1996). 19 Apr. 2001 <www.hull.ac.uk/renforum/v1no1/clare.htm>.

Article, No Author listed

"People: Your Greatest Asset." <u>Human Resources</u>. 15 July 1999. 11 Sept. 2000 <http://netscape/business/humanresources>.

E-mail

Butterill, Chris. "Italics Versus Underlining in MLA Style." E-mail to the author. 25 Mar. 2002.

Encyclopedia Article Online

"Coleridge, Samuel Taylor." <u>Encyclopedia Britannica Online</u>. Vers. 99.1. 1994–99. Encyclopedia Britannica. 19 Aug. 2001 <www.eb.com/bol/topic?eu=25136&sctn=1>.

Film, Video, or Film Clip Online

"A Light Still Bright: Video on the Ecumenical Patriarchate of Constantinople." <u>The History of the Orthodox Christian Church</u>. 1996. GoTelecom Online. 24 Aug. 2001 <www.goarch.org/goa/departments/gotel/online_videos. html#LIGHT>.

Government Document

Canada. Parliament. House of Commons. <u>Plans and Priorities 2001–2002 (RPP) of the House of Commons Administration</u> 18 May 2001. 11 July 2001 <www.parl.gc.ca/information/ about/process/house/plans01/01-toc-e.htm>.

Canada. <u>Youth Criminal Justice Act</u>, Bill C-3, First Reading, 14 Oct. 1999 (36th Parl., 2nd sess.). 19 Sept. 2001 <www.parl.gc.ca/36/2/parlbus/chambus/house/bills/ government/C-3/C-3_1/C-3TOCE.html>.

9c

Canada. House of Commons. Standing Committee on Canadian
Heritage. <u>The Challenge of Change: A Consideration of the</u>
<u>Canadian Book Industry: Report of the Standing Committee</u>
<u>on Canadian Heritage.</u> Ottawa: Public Works and Government
Services Canada, June 2000. 11 July 2001 <www.cmhc-schl.
gc.ca/en/index.cfm?pMenu=72>.

Home Page for a Website

Dawe, James. <u>Jane Austen Page</u>. 1996–2000. 15 May 2000
<www.jamesdawe.com>.

Magazine Article Online

Fuchs, Pablo. "Worry-Free Water." <u>Canadian Business</u> 25 June
2001. 27 June 2001 <www.canadianbusiness.com/
magazine_items/2001/june25_01_freewater.shtml>.

Magazine Article Online, No Author Listed

"Winners 2001: The Best Product Designs of the Year!" <u>Business Week</u>
25 June 2001. 1 July 2001 <www.businessweek.com/
magazine/content/01_26/b3738084.htm>.

Miscellaneous Internet Sources

List the type of work for such items as a cartoon, map, chart, advertisement,
and so forth, as shown in this example:

Pearson. "Vancouver Experiences Earthquake." Cartoon. <u>CBC News</u>
<u>Online</u>. 6 Mar. 2001. 10 Mar. 2001 <http://cbc.ca/news/>.

MOO, MUD, and Chat Rooms

"Virtual Conference on Mary Shelley's <u>The Last Man</u>." Villa Diodati
at EmoryMOO. 13 Sept. 1997. 24 Aug. 2000
<www.rc.umd.edu/villa/vc97/Shelley_9_13_97.html>.

Chat rooms are seldom useful for scholarly research, but if you find information you wish to cite, use this form:

"Australia: The Olympics 2000." 30 May 2000. <u>Yahoo! Chat</u>.
30 May 2000 <http://chat.yahoo.com/
?room=Australia::160032654&identity=chat>.

Newsgroups, Listserv and Usenet News

Camilleri, Rosemary. "Narrative Bibliography." 10 Mar. 1997. Online
posting. H-Rhetoric. 11 Mar. 2000 <H-RHETOR@msu.edu>.
Link, Richard. "Territorial Fish." Online Posting. 11 Jan. 1997.
Environment Newsgroup. 11 Mar. 2000 <www.rec.aquaria.
freshwater.misc>.

Newspaper Article, Column, Editorial Online

Fotheringham, Allan. "Dalton Camp Front-Room Boy." <u>Globe and Mail</u>
23 Mar 2002. 25 Mar 2002 <www.theglobeandmail.com/servlet/
HTMLTemplate?tf=tgam/columnists/Summary.html&cf=tgam/

9c

> common/MiniHub.cfg&configFileLoc=tgam/
> config&hub=allanFotheringham&title=Allan_Fotheringham>.

Posting for E-mail Discussion Groups

List the Internet site if known; otherwise show the e-mail address of the list's moderator.

> Chapman, David. "Reforming the Tax and Benefit System to
>   Reduce Unemployment." Online Posting. 25 Feb. 1998.
>   Democracy Design Forum. 27 May 2000
>   <chapman@democdesignforumj.demon.co.uk>.

Scholarly Project or Archive

> Victorian Women Writers Project. Ed. Perry Willett. Apr. 1997.
>   Indiana U. 4 Jan. 1998 <www.indiana.edu/~letrs/vwwp>.

Bibliography Form—Databases

A database by a national vendor, such as DIALOG, is a massive collection of data arranged by discipline or subject. Provide the name and identifying numbers to the entry:

> Bowles, M. D. "The Organization Man Goes to College: AT&T's
>   Experiment in Humanistic Education, 1953–60." The
>   Historian 61 (1998): 15+. DIALOG database (#88, IAC
>   Business A.R.T.S., Item 04993186). 19 May 2000.

Database Article at a Library's Online Service with a Listed URL

Most libraries have converted their computer searches to online databases, such as *LEXIS-NEXIS, ProQuest Direct, EBSCOhost, Electric Library,* and *InfoTrac.* If the source provides the URL, omit the identifying numbers for the database or the keyword used in the search and include the URL. Here's an example from *InfoTrac*:

> Lee, Catherine C. "The South in Toni Morrison's Song of Solomon:
>   Initiation, Healing, and Home." Studies in the Literary
>   Imagination 31 (1998): 109–23. Abstract. 19 Sept. 2001
>   <http://firstsearch.oclc.org/next=NEXTCMD>.

Database Article from an Online Service to Which You Personally Subscribe

Many students research topics from their homes, where they use such services as AOL Canada or Netscape. If the URL is provided, use the form of this next example.

> "Nutrition and Cancer." Discovery Health 1 May 2000. 3 Aug. 2000
>   <www.discoveryhealth.com/Sc000/8096/164609.html>.

Bibliography Form—CD-ROM Sources

CD-ROM technology provides information in five different ways, and each method of transmission requires an adjustment in the form of the "Works Cited" or "Sources Cited" entry.

9c

Abstract

> Figueredo, Aurelio J., and Laura Ann McCloskey. "Sex, Money, and
> Paternity: The Evolutionary Psychology of Domestic
> Violence." <u>Ethnology and Sociobiology</u> 14 (1993): 353–79.
> Abstract. <u>PsycINFO</u>. CD-ROM. Silverplatter. 12 Jan. 1999.

Articles, Full-Text with Publication Information for Printed Source

Full-text articles are available from national distributors, such as Information
Access Company (*InfoTrac*), UMI-ProQuest (*ProQuest*), *Silverplatter,* or *SIRS*
CD-ROM Information Systems.

> "Faulkner Biography." <u>Discovering Authors</u>. CD-ROM. Detroit:
> Gale, 1999.

Book, Complete Text

> Poe, Edgar Allan. "Fall of the House of Usher." <u>Electronic Classical
> Library</u>. CD-ROM. Garden Grove, CA: World Library, 1999.

Encyclopedia

> "NFB Wins Oscar." <u>Canadian Encyclopedia World Edition</u>. CD-ROM.
> McClelland and Stewart. 1999.

Note: When you cite from electronic sources, complete information may
not be readily available—for example, the original publication data may be
missing. In such cases, provide what is available.

Bibliography Form—Other Sources

Advertisement

> PGA Tour. Advertisement. ESPN. 14 Feb. 2002.
> WestJet. Billboard advertisement. Saskatoon, SK. Aug. 2002.

9c

Art Work

If you actually experience the work itself, use the form shown below:

> Jackson, Alexander Young. <u>Grain Elevators</u>. Winchester Galleries,
> Victoria, BC.

If the art work is a special showing at a museum, use the form of this next
example.

> "Gertrude Vanderbilt Whitney: Printmakers' Patron." Whitney
> Museum of American Art, New York. 22 Feb. 1995.

Use this next form to cite reproductions in books and journals.

> Raphael. <u>School of Athens</u>. The Vatican, Rome. <u>The World Book-
> Encyclopedia</u>. 1976 ed.

Broadcast Interview

> "Margaret Atwood." Interview with Carol Off. <u>The Magazine</u>. CBC.
> CFWH, Whitehorse. 4 Sept. 2001.

Bulletin

French, Earl. <u>Personal Problems in Industrial Research and Development</u>. Bulletin No. 51. Ithaca: New York State School of Industrial and Labor Relations, 1993.

Cartoon

Mosher, Terry. Cartoons. <u>Maclean's</u> 16 July 2001: 24.

If you cannot decipher the name of the cartoonist, omit it.

Computer Software

<u>Study Smart: Study Skills Software for Students</u>. Computer software. Whitby: McGraw-Hill Ryerson, 1997.

Conference Proceedings

Bonin, Daniel, ed. <u>Towards Reconciliation?: The Language Issue in Canada in the 1990s</u>. Proceedings of a Conference Jointly Organized with the École de Droit, Université de Moncton, Dec. 1989. Kingston: Queen's University, Institute of Intergovernmental Relations, 1992.

Dissertation, Unpublished

Graham, Catherine E. "Dramaturgy and Community-Building in Canadian Popular Theatre: English Canadian, Québécois, and Native Approaches." Diss. McGill U, 1997.

Film, Videocassette or DVD

Cite title, director, distributor, and year.

<u>The Red Violin</u>. Dir. François Girard. Telefilm Canada, 1998.

If the film is a DVD, videocassette, filmstrip, slide program, or videodisc, add the type of medium before the name of the distributor.

<u>A Beautiful Mind</u>. Dir. Ron Howard. DVD. Universal Pictures, 2002.

9c

Interview, Unpublished

For an interview that you conduct, name the person interviewed, the type of interview (e.g., telephone interview, personal interview, e-mail interview), and the date.

Michaels, Donald. Telephone interview. 25 Mar. 2002.

Letter, Personal

Aire, Jayne. Letter to the author. 5 Aug. 2001.

Letter, Published

Eisenhower, Dwight. Letter to Richard Nixon. 20 Apr. 1968. <u>Memoirs of Richard Nixon</u>. By Richard Nixon. New York: Grosset, 1978.

Map

County Boundaries and Names. United States Base Map GE-50,
    No. 86. Washington, DC: GPO, 1987.
Eastern Nova Scotia–Cape Breton Island. Map. Montreal: Reader's
    Digest Association (Canada), 1995.

Microfilm or Microfiche

Chapman, Dan. "Panel Could Help Protect Children." Winston-
    Salem Journal 14 Jan. 1990: 14. Newsbank: Welfare and
    Social Problems 12 (1990): fiche 1, grids A8–11.
Tuckerman, H. T. "James Fenimore Cooper." Microfilm. North
    American Review 89 (1959): 298–316.

Mimeographed Material

Butterill, Christine A. "Précis, Paraphrasing and Plagiarism."
    Mimeographed material. Winnipeg: U of Manitoba, 2002.

Musical Composition

Mozart, Wolfgang A. Jupiter. Symphony No. 41.

Treat a published score as you would a book.

Legrenzi, Giovanni. "La Buscha." Sonata for Instruments.
    Historical Anthology of Music. Ed. Archibald T. Davison and
    Willi Apel. Cambridge, MA: Harvard UP, 1950. 70–76.

Pamphlet

Treat pamphlets as you would a book.

Manitoba Community Wellness Working Group. First Nation
    Community Wellness Diploma. Winnipeg, MB: Author, n.d.

Performance

9c

Cite a play, opera, ballet, or concert as you would a film, but include the site
(normally the theatre and city) and the date of the performance.

The Contract. National Ballet of Canada. Hummingbird Centre for
    the Performing Arts, Toronto. 16 May 2002.

If your text emphasizes the work of a particular individual, begin with the
appropriate name:

Tovey, Bramwell, cond. Inspector Tovey and the VSO Investigate—
    Sweet Harmony. Vancouver Symphony Orchestra. Orpheum
    Theatre, Vancouver. 9 June 2002.

Posters and Programs

"Canadian Expert Lectures on Women and Work." Poster. Madison.
    27 Mar. 2000.
"Gospel Arts Day." Program. Nashville: Fisk U. 18 June 1997.

Public Address or Lecture

Identify the nature of the address (e.g., Lecture, Reading), include the site (normally the lecture hall and city), and the date of the performance.

> Hill, Christopher. "Beatty Memorial Lecture: Milton and the English Revolution." Faculty of Graduate Studies, McGill U, Montreal. 26 Nov. 1987.

Recording on Record, Tape, or Disc

If you are not citing a compact disc, indicate the medium (e.g., audio cassette, audiotape [reel-to-reel tape], or LP [long-playing record]).

> "Chaucer: The Nun's Priest's Tale." <u>Canterbury Tales</u>. Narr. in Middle English by Robert Ross. Audio cassette. Caedmon, 1971.
> John, Elton. "Candle in the Wind." <u>Goodbye Yellow Brick Road</u>. LP. MCA, 1974.

Report

Titles of unbound reports are placed within quotation marks; bound reports are treated as books:

> The Bureau of Tobacco Control. <u>Report on Tobacco Control</u>. Ottawa: Health Canada, 1999.

Reproductions and Photographs

> Carr, Emily. "A Haida Village." Reproduction in <u>History of the Canadian Peoples</u>. By Alvin Finkle and Margaret Conrad. Toronto: Copp Clark Pitman, 1993. 451.

Table, Illustration, Chart, or Graph

Tables or illustrations of any kind published within works need a detailed citation:

> Abken, Peter A. "Over-the-Counter Financial Derivatives: Risky Business?" Chart No. 2. <u>Economic Review</u> 79.2 (Mar.–Apr. 1994): 7.
> "The Human Genetic Code." Illustration. <u>Facts on File</u> 29 June 2000: 437–38.

Television or Radio Program

If available or relevant, provide information in this order: the episode (in quotation marks), the title of the program (underlined or italicized), title of the series (neither underlined or italicized nor in quotation marks), name of the network, call letters and city of the local station, and the broadcast date. Add other information (such as narrator) after the episode or program narrated or directed or performed. Place the number of episodes, if relevant, before the title of the series.

> "George Knudson." Narr. Rod Black. <u>Profile</u>. TSN. Toronto. 16 Mar 2001.

9c

"Remembering Mordecai Richler." Narr. Alison Smith. <u>The National</u>. CBC-TV. CBWT, Winnipeg. 3 July 2001.

Thesis

Nielsen, Robert F. "A Barely Perceptible Limp: The First World War in Canadian Fiction (1914–1939)." Thesis. U of Guelph, 1971.

Transparency

Fraser, Lisa. <u>Making Your Mark: Teaching Overhead Package</u>. 54 transparencies, 99 overlays. Port Perry, ON: LDF, 1996.

Unpublished Paper

James, Neil. "Perception of the Inuit Culture by Western Civilization." Unpublished paper. Winnipeg, 2002.

Videotape

<u>No Turning Back: The Royal Commission on Aboriginal Peoples</u>. Videocassette. National Film Board of Canada, 1997.

Thompson, Paul. "W. B. Yeats." Lecture. Video cassette. Memphis U, 1995.

Voice Mail

Milne, Marlene. "Memo to Mochnacz." Voice mail to the author. 25 Feb. 2002.

9d Formatting the Paper in MLA Style

The format of a research paper consists of the following parts:

1. Title page or opening page with title
2. Outline (if required)
3. Text of the paper
4. Content notes (optional)
5. Appendix (optional)
6. Works cited or Sources Cited

Title Page or Opening Page

A research paper in MLA style does not need a separate title page unless you include an outline, abstract, or other introductory matter. Place your identification in the upper left corner of your opening page, and centre your title as follows:

James 1

Neil James
032.124 Native Studies
Professor C. G. Trott
February 17, 2002

Perception of the Inuit Culture by Western Civilization

Many instructors, however, require a title page; therefore you should check with them as to their preference. Centre the information uniformly in the middle of the title page, and place the running head (the page number typed after your last name, e.g., "James 1") in the top right-hand corner of the page, as in the following example:

James 1

Perception of the Inuit Culture by Western Civilization

by
Neil James

032.124 Native Studies
Professor C. G. Trott
February 17, 2002

Note that the writer's last name, in this case *James*, is the running head in MLA style and would be the optional running head in CMS (see Chapter 12). Use a shortened version of your title, rather than your name, as the running head in both APA and CBE styles (see Chapters 10 and 11).

Outline

Include your outline with the finished manuscript only if your instructor requires it. Place it after the title page on separate pages, and number these pages with small Roman numerals, beginning with ii (e.g., ii, iii, iv, v) at the top right hand corner of the page, just after your last name (e.g., James iii).

For details on writing an outline, see 5d, pages 40–42, and for additional information on numbering pages and running heads, see the Appendix.

Text of the Paper

Double space throughout your entire paper. In general, you should *not* use subtitles or numbered divisions for your paper, even if it becomes 20 pages long. Instead, use continuous paragraphing without subdivisions or headings. MLA style calls for present tense. (See 10b, page 118, for a discussion that compares tense in MLA and APA styles.)

If the closing page of your text runs short, leave the remainder of the page blank. Do not write "The End" or provide artwork as a closing signal. Do not start "Notes", or "Works Cited" or "Sources Cited" on this final page of text; place them on separate pages at the end of the paper.

Content Endnotes Page

Label this page with the word "Notes" centred one inch from the top edge of the sheet, at least one double space below your page number. Number the notes in sequence to match those within your text. Double space throughout.

Appendix

An appendix precedes the "Works Cited" or "Sources Cited" list. This is the logical location for tables and illustrations, computer data, questionnaire results,

9d

complicated statistics, mathematical proofs, or detailed descriptions of special equipment. Double space appendixes and begin each appendix on a new sheet. Continue your page numbering sequence in the upper right corner.

Works Cited or Sources Cited

Centre the heading "Works Cited" or "Sources Cited" one inch from the top edge of the sheet. Continue the page numbering sequence in the upper right corner. Double space throughout. Use a hanging indention, that is, set the first line of each entry flush left and indent subsequent lines five spaces. For examples, see the "Sources Cited" page at the end of the following sample paper.

9e Sample Paper in MLA Style

The following paper demonstrates the correct form of a research paper in MLA style. Note that the writer's instructor may have requested that her paper be submitted using the traditional footnote system. Consult Chapter 12, pages 156–162, to see how "Breaking the Mould" would be written using the Chicago footnote system.

9e

Most instructors require a title page. The running head will appear at the top of each page.

Senyk 1

**Breaking the Mould:
Artemisia Gentileschi's Contribution to Art**

by

Katrina A. T. Senyk

**54.124 Art History
Dr. M. Steggles
March 10, 2002**

Senyk 2

Many people believe that artists view the human condition from the unique perspective of their individuality and unconsciously illustrate their perspective via their art, in much the same way that "personality theories are strongly influenced by personal and subjective factors [. . .] [and] reflect the biographies of their authors" (Hergenhahn and Olson 569). If this is so, then artists' perceptions of the world are translated into their works of art. Moreover, Mary Garrard states that, historically, the "assignment of sex roles has created fundamental differences between the sexes in their perception, experience, and expectations of the world [. . .] that cannot help but be carried over into the creative process" (202).

Artemisia Gentileschi (1593–c.1652) portrayed her subjects from her unusual perspective as a female artist in the 17th century. Viewers frequently question why Gentileschi painted such powerful female protagonists; by examining Gentileschi's perception of her world, the viewer can better understand what her art represented to her as a woman in a male-dominated profession. Gentileschi's work explores women's demands to be justly represented.

In the 17th century, options for women were limited to marrying and raising children, or devotion to the Catholic Church as a nun. Alternatives were not viewed as appropriate. However, Artemisia Gentileschi was more fortunate than her peers; having been born to a painter, she was raised in "an environment where she could acquire the basic skills necessary for a professional artist" (Slatkin 49). Although it was "difficult for women to become artists during this time . . . [Gentileschi] was able to gain access to a world that would normally have been forbidden" (Corbell and Guy).

Katrina identifies the issue and cites sources in her opening to confirm the serious nature of the discussion. See pages 79–81 for details about writing the introduction.

Katrina expresses her thesis in a sentence at the end of the introduction.

9e

Note that the reference to Corbell and Guy lacks a page number because it is an Internet source (see pages 102–105).

Her father, Orazio, one of the first followers of Caravaggio, trained Gentileschi from an early age, but he recognized his limits as a teacher when her talent surpassed his (Slatkin 49). Orazio hired Agostino Tassi to tutor her in perspective, but the perspective Tassi imparted to Gentileschi had nothing to do with any artistic technique. During one of his "lessons," Tassi raped her, and continued sexual relations with promises of marriage. However, when it became apparent that Tassi had no intention of marrying Gentileschi, Orazio sued Tassi for ruining her honour (Slatkin 49).

During the early 17th century, as Spear notes:

legal and social dimensions of violent rape centred on questions of family and marriage-ability, in which women resembled (male) property for exchange . . . usually poor girls sought not the rapist's imprisonment, but either his hand in marriage or payment of a dowry. . . . Marriage, it must be emphasized, rather than rape, was the core substance of the litigation. (570)

Gentileschi, as an unmarried woman, was classified as "damaged property." She was subjected to torture, a humiliating public trial, and a medical examination to prove that she was a virgin before the rape (Corbell and Guy). The sexual assaults, compounded by the ordeal of the trial, no doubt caused a "crystallizing moment of recognition of sexuality and gender power" in Gentileschi (Pollock 503).

The emotional chaos resulting from the assaults and the trial is most likely expressed in Gentileschi's work <u>Judith Decapitating Holofernes</u>, painted shortly after the trial was dismissed (Corbell and Guy). Gentileschi's interpretation of this biblical story is particularly gruesome; she uses vivid colours, indicating strong, vehement emotion and enhancing the sense of violence and movement (Corbell and Guy). This painting is clearly a "cathartic expression of the artist's private, and perhaps repressed, rage" (Spear 569); "the violence her Judith wreaks on Holofernes is strongly suggestive of the turmoil she must have been experiencing" (Corbell and Guy).

Margin note: Long quotations are indented one inch or 10 spaces. The page number is placed outside the final period (see page 91).

Margin tab: 9e

Senyk 4

Caravaggio also depicts this scene in his <u>Judith and Holofernes</u>. Both artists depict the moment when Judith severs Holofernes' head, but Caravaggio positions the figures across the picture surface, weakening the overall effect; the characters seem less active in decapitating Holofernes and more like passive witnesses. Gentileschi, instead, chooses to intersect the arms of all three figures in the centre of the picture plane, "fixing the viewer's attention inescapably on the grisly act much more convincing[ly] than Caravaggio" (Slatkin 51). Caravaggio depicts Judith as a weak, ineffective female, drawing back distastefully, almost cringing at the sight of blood, whereas Gentileschi's Judith looks "as if she is [angrily] struggling to pull the sword through Holofernes' [neck]" (Corbell and Guy). Perhaps Gentileschi is expressing the anger she feels about her helplessness and vulnerability as a woman.

[A portion of this paper has been omitted.]

With a new perspective on the world after the experiences of the sexual assaults and the charade of a trial, Artemisia Gentileschi went on to develop her unique style combining dynamic, gruesome naturalism with innovative interpretations of typical Renaissance and Baroque themes. "She adapted some of Caravaggio's devices to forge an original style of strength and beauty. She expressed her identity as a woman and as an artist" (Slatkin 54). As a woman, Gentileschi identified with the plight of the heroine, whereas her male colleagues identified with the villain's anticipated pleasure.

Artemisia Gentileschi's great contribution to art is found in the "categorically different treatment of major themes around the well-established topos of the heroic woman" (Pollock 50). Because most artists and patrons have historically been men, naturally most paintings would represent the perspective of the male; and as Garrard notes, "[men have been] drawn by instinct to identify more with the villain than with the heroine" (194).

9e

Katrina now advances her conclusion. See pages 82–83 for details.

As a result of her experiences, Gentileschi began to reinterpret traditional themes from the viewpoint of the dynamic, assertive female protagonist. In her television documentary, <u>Artemisia</u>, Adrienne Clarkson asserts that this artist "(broke) the constraints of her female condition to become arguably the most remarkable woman painter of the post-modern period." Through her body of work, Gentileschi explores in depth women's demands to be justly represented.

9e

9e Sample Paper in MLA Style **117**

Senyk 6

Sources Cited

See 9c for details on the form for citations in MLA style.

Artemisia. Narr. and Dir. Adrienne Clarkson. <u>Adrienne
    Clarkson Presents.</u> CBC–TV. CBWT, Winnipeg. 25
    Jan. 1993.

Corbell, Rebecca, and Samantha Guy. "Artemisia
    Gentileschi and the Age of Baroque" 1995. 25
    Feb. 2001 <http://rubens.anu.edu.au/
    student.projects/artemisia/Artemisia.html>.

Garrard, Mary. <u>Artemisia Gentileschi: The Image of the
    Female Hero in Italian Baroque Art</u>. Princeton:
    Princeton UP, 1989.

Hergenhahn, B. R., and Matthew H. Olson. <u>An
    Introduction to Theories of Personality</u>. 5th ed.
    Toronto: Prentice Hall Canada, 1999.

Pollock, Griselda. Rev. of <u>Artemisia Gentileschi: The
    Image of the Female Hero in Italian Baroque Art</u>,
    by Mary Garrard. <u>Art Bulletin</u> 72 (1990):
    499–505.

Slatkin, Wendy. <u>Women Artists in History: From
    Antiquity to the Present</u>. Toronto: Prentice-Hall
    Canada, 1990.

Spear, Richard. "Artemisia Gentileschi: Ten Years of
    Fact and Fiction." <u>Art Bulletin</u> 82 (2000):
    568–79.

Katrina's bibliography demonstrates the citation form for books, journal articles, an Internet source, and a television program.

9e

10 Using APA Style

You may be required to write a research paper in APA style, which is governed by the *Publication Manual of the American Psychological Association*. This style has gained wide acceptance in academic circles. APA style is used in psychology and the other social sciences, and versions similar to it are used in business and the biological and earth sciences.

The American Psychological Association has established websites that, among other things, explain its method for citing electronic sources. This chapter conforms to the stipulations of the fifth edition of the APA style manual with adjustments based on APA's current websites. Consult **www.apastyle.org/elecref.html** and **www.apastyle.org/faqs.html**.

10a Establishing a Critical Approach

In scientific writing, the thesis (see pages 6–7) usually takes a different form. It appears as a *hypothesis* or *statement of principle*. The hypothesis is a theory that needs testing and analysis, which you will do as part of your research. It is an idea expressed as a truth for the purpose of argument and investigation. It makes a prediction based upon the theory. Here is an example:

> It was predicted that patients who suffer a compulsive bulimic disorder would have a more disrupted family life.

In a similar fashion, the statement of principle makes a declaration in defence of an underlying but unstated theory, as shown here:

> The most effective recall cue is the one that is encoded within the event that is to be remembered.

Your work would attempt to prove this principle. Be careful to avoid false assumptions in your hypothesis or statement of principle (see page 6).

10b Writing in the Proper Tense for an APA Style Paper

Verb tense is an indicator that distinguishes papers in the humanities from those in the natural and social sciences. MLA style uses the present tense when you refer to a cited work ("Kozyrskyj *stipulates*" or "the work of Johnson and Stewart *shows*"). In contrast, APA style uses the past tense or present perfect tense ("Kozyrskyj *stipulated*" or "the work of Johnson and Stewart *has demon-*

strated"). The APA style does require present tense when you discuss the results (e.g., "*the results confirm*" or "*the study indicates*") and when you mention established knowledge (e.g., "*the therapy offers some hope*" or "*salt contributes to hypertension*"). This example shows correct usage for APA style:

> Howes et al. (1996) **found** that few clinical psychology supervisors in Canada received sufficient formal training; Johnson and Stewart (2000) **have reported** similar findings.

However, as shown in the next example, use the present tense (*do not have*) for established knowledge. The past tense (*conducted*) is correct for a reference to completed research.

> Psychologists in Canada **do not have** prescription privileges; Walters (2001) **conducted** a meta-analysis of opinion survey data on this issue.

10c   Blending Sources into Your Writing

The APA style uses these conventions for in-text citations.

- Cite last names only.
- Cite the year, within parentheses, immediately after the name of the author.
- Cite page numbers always with a direct quotation, seldom with a paraphrase.
- Use "p." or "pp." before page numbers.

Citing Last Name Only and the Year of Publication

An in-text citation in APA style requires the last name of the author and the year of publication.

> Montague (2000) has advanced the idea of combining the social sciences and mathematics to chart human behaviour.

If you do not use the author's name in your text, place the name(s) within the parenthetical citation followed by a comma and the year.

> One study has advanced the idea of combining the social sciences and mathematics to chart human behaviour (Montague, 2000).

Providing a Page Number

If you quote the exact words of a source, provide a page number and *do use* "p." or "pp." Place the page number in one of two places: after the year or at the end of the quotation.

> Montague (2000) has advanced the idea of "soft mathematics," which is the practice of "applying mathematics to study people's behaviour" (p. B4).

Citing a Block of Material

Present a quotation of 40 words or more as a separate block, indented five to seven spaces, or one-half inch from the left margin. (*Note:* MLA style uses 10

10c

spaces or one inch.) Because the quotation is set off from the text in a distinctive block, do not enclose it with quotation marks. Do not single space. Do not indent the first line an extra five spaces; however, do indent the first line of any additional paragraphs that appear in the block an extra five spaces, that is, 10 spaces from the left margin. Set parenthetical citations outside the last period.

> Johnson and Stewart (2000) reported that:
>> Canadian programs and internship sites have failed to adequately prepare students to undertake a central professional demand (clinical supervisory responsibilities).
>> However, although relatively few respondents received training in supervision, those who did have such training appear to have benefited from it. (pp. 314–315)

Citing a Work with More Than One Author

When one work has two or more authors, use *and* in the text, but use *&* in the citation.

> Battiste and Barman (1995) stressed the importance of spirituality in Aboriginal education.

but

> It has been emphasized (Battiste & Barman, 1995) that spirituality is central to the education of Aboriginal children.

For three to five authors, name them all in the first entry (e.g., Torgerson, Andrews, Smith, Lawrence, & Dunlap, 2001), but thereafter use "et al." (e.g., Torgerson et al., 2001). For six or more authors, employ "et al." in the first and in all subsequent instances (e.g., Fredericks et al., 2001).

Citing More Than One Work by an Author

Use lowercase letters (a, b, c) to identify two or more works published in the same year by the same author, for example, (Thompson, 2001a) and (Thompson, 2001b). Then use "2001a" and "2001b" in your list of references. (See "Author, Two or More Works by the Same Author, page 124, for an example). If necessary, specify additional information:

10c

> Horton (2000; cf. Thomas, 1999a, p. 89, and 1999b, p. 426) suggested an intercorrelation of these testing devices. But after multiple-group analysis, Welston (1998, esp. p. 211) reached an opposite conclusion.

Citing Two or More Works by Different Authors

List two or more works by different authors in alphabetical order by the surname of the first author cited:

> Several studies (Baer and Lambert, 1995; Lennard 1987; Nakhaie & Brym 1999) have investigated the political attitudes of professors in Canadian universities.

Citing Indirect Sources

Use a double reference to cite somebody who has been quoted in a book or an article. That is, use the original author(s) in the text and cite your source for the information in the parenthetical citation.

> In other research, Massie and Rosenthal (1997) studied home movies of children diagnosed with autism, but determining criteria was difficult due to the differences in quality and dating of the available videotapes (cited in Osterling & Dawson, 1998, p. 248).

Citing from a Textbook or Anthology

If you make an in-text citation to an article or chapter of a textbook, casebook, or anthology, use the in-text citation to refer only to the person(s) you cite; the References page will clarify the nature of this citation to Tanner. (See "Component Part of an Anthology," page 125.)

> One writer described the Innu of Labrador as a "threatened people" (Tanner, 2000, p. 75).

Abbreviating Corporate Authors in the Text

Corporate authors may be abbreviated after a first, full reference:

> One group has actively lobbied the Canadian government to label alcoholic beverages as hazardous if consumed during pregnancy (Canadian Medical Association [CMA], 2000).

Thereafter, refer to the corporate author by initials: (CMA, 2000).

Citing a Work with an Anonymous Author

When a work has no author listed, cite the title as part of the in-text citation or use the first few words of the material.

> The cost per individual student has continued to rise rapidly ("Money Concerns," 1998, p. 2).

However, when a work's author is identified as "Anonymous," use this form:

> It has been shown that student expenses can be expected to rise for the next several years (Anonymous, 2002).

10c

Citing Personal Communications

The *Publication Manual of the American Psychological Association* stipulates that personal communications, (e-mail, telephone conversations, interviews, memos, and conversations) which others cannot retrieve, should be cited in the text only and not mentioned at all in the references list (bibliography). In the in-text citation, give the initials as well as the last name of the source, provide the date, and briefly describe the nature of the communication.

> B. A. Frost (personal communication, August 24, 2001) described the potential adverse effects of herbal products.

Citing Electronic Sources

In most cases, omit page numbers for articles you find on the Internet. Monitors differ, as do printers, so do not count pages on the screen and do not use the page numbers of your printouts. Electronic text is searchable, so readers can find your quotation quickly with the Find feature of a browser after locating the Internet address in your References list. However, if an article on the Internet has numbered paragraphs, by all means supply that information in your citation. (Jones, 2001, ¶5) or (Jones, 2001, para.5).

> The most common type of diabetes is non-insulin-dependent-diabetes mellitus (NIDDM), which "affects 90% of those with diabetes and usually appears after age 40" (Larson, 1996, para. 3).

Abstract

> "Psychologically oriented techniques used to elicit confessions may undermine their validity" (Kassim, 1997, abstract).

Aggregated Database on a Server or CD-ROM

> *The Canadian Encyclopedia Plus* (2001) has described social sciences as a category of disciplines which include anthropology, economics, political science, psychology, and sociology, and sometimes criminology, education, geography, law, psychiatry, philosophy, [and] religion.

E-mail

Treat e-mail as a personal communication, cited only in the text and not in the bibliography. However, electronic chat groups have gained legitimacy in recent years, so in the text give the exact date and e-mail address *only* if the citation has scholarly relevance and *only* if the author has made public the e-mail address with the expressed wish for correspondence.

> One technical writing instructor (March 8, 1997) has bemoaned the inability of hardware developers to maintain pace with the ingenuity of software developers. In his e-mail message, he indicated that educational institutions cannot keep pace with the hardware developers. Thus, "students nationwide suffer with antiquated equipment, even though it's only a few years old" (ClemmerJ@APSU01.APSU.EDU).

10c

If the e-mail is part of a network or online journal, it *may* be listed in the bibliography. In such cases, use the form shown on page 123 under "Listserv."

Government Document

> The website *Herbal and Homeopathic Products* (1998) has provided the report of the Canadian Pharmacists Association's Advisory Panel on Herbal Remedies, in which 10 recommendations are made to the House of Commons Standing Committee on Health.

Listserv (E-mail Discussion Group)

Chang (February 14, 2002) has recommended the book *Canadian Guidelines for Sexual Health Education* as a helpful resource for teachers.

Online Magazine

Canadian Geographic (2001) contended that Toronto is "arguably the most multicultural city in the world."

Website

Carpentier (2000), who teaches a graduate course on government information at McGill University, stressed that "a knowledge of the organization and functions of governments is required for an understanding of government publications and information."

10d Writing the List of References in APA Style

Use the title "References" for your bibliography page. Alphabetize the entries and double space throughout. Every reference used in your text should appear in your alphabetical list of references at the end of the paper. An exception to this rule exists for untraceable sources like e-mail, personal letters, and phone conversations. Identify these sources in your text, as explained in "E-mail" on page 122.

Use the hanging indentation shown below when preparing your reference list. Type the first line of each flush left, and indent succeeding lines five spaces or one half inch. Italicize names of books, periodicals, and volume numbers, as shown in the next example:

Whittaker, J.C. (2000). Alonia and Dhoukanes: The ethnoarcheology of threshing in Cyprus. *Near Eastern Archaeologist, 63*. Retrieved June 26, 2001, from www.asor.org/nea/632.pdf

Bibliography Form—Books

Enter information for books in the following order. Items 1, 3, and 8 are required; add other items according to the rules that follow:

1. **Author**
2. Chapter or part of the book
3. **Title of the book**
4. Editor, translator, or compiler
5. Edition
6. Volume number of the book
7. Name of the series
8. **Place, publisher, and date**
9. Page numbers
10. Total number of volumes

10d

The following list explains and gives examples of the correct form for books and parts of books.

Author

> Thadani, M. B. (1999). *Herbal remedies: Weeding fact from fiction*. Winnipeg: Cantext.

List the author (surname first with initials for given names), year of publication within parentheses, title of the book italicized with *only* the first word of the title and any subtitle capitalized (but do capitalize proper nouns), place of publication, and publisher. In the publisher's name, omit the words *Publishing, Company,* or *Inc.,* but otherwise give a full name: Victoria University Press, Pearson Education Canada, HarperCollins. Indent the second line five spaces, or use the tab key for whatever indentation your computer font provides.

Authors, Two to Six

Give surnames and initials for up to six authors:

> Castellano, M. B., Davis, L., & Lahache, L. (Eds.). (2000). *Aboriginal education: Fulfilling the promise*. Vancouver: UBC Press.

For seven or more, give surnames and initials for the first six authors; thereafter, use "et al.," which means "and others" (not italicized and with a period after "al").

Author, Two or More Works by the Same Author

List chronologically, not alphabetically, two or more works by the same author; for example, Fitzgerald's 1997 publication would precede his 1998 publication.

> Fitzgerald, R. F. (1997). *Water samples* . . . .
> Fitzgerald, R. F. (1998). *Controlling* . . . .

References to the same author in the same year are alphabetized and marked with lower case letters—a, b, c—immediately after the date:

> Cobb, R. A. (1990a). *Circulating systems* . . . .
> Cobb, R. A. (1990b). *Delay valves* . . . .

10d

Author, Anonymous

If no author is listed, begin with the title of the article.

> Canadian expatriates in show business. (2000). *The Canadian Encyclopedia*. New York: Harper.

Author, Corporation or Institution

List author, year, title of the work (italicized), place, and publisher. Use the word *Author* when the publisher and the author are the same.

> Canadian Psychological Association. (2001). *Practice guidelines for providers of psychological services* (3rd ed.). Ottawa: Author.

Component Part of Anthology, Textbook, or Collection

List author(s), date, chapter or section title, editor (with name in normal order) preceded by "In" and followed by "(Ed.)" or "(Eds.)," the name of the book (italicized), page numbers to the specific section of the book cited (placed within parentheses), place of publication, and publisher.

> Tanner, A. (2000). The Innu of Labrador, Canada. In M. M. Freeman
> (Ed.), *Endangered peoples of the Arctic: Struggles to survive
> and thrive* (pp. 75–92). Westport, CT: Greenwood Press.

Cross-References to Works in an Anthology, Textbook or Collection

Make a primary reference to the anthology, textbook, or collection:

> Vesterman, W. (Ed.). (1991). *Readings for the 21st Century*. Boston:
> Allyn & Bacon.

Thereafter, make cross references to the primary source, in this case to Vesterman, as in the following examples:

> Bailey, J. (1988). Jobs for women in the nineties. In Vesterman,
> pp. 55–63.
> Fallows, D. (1982). Why mothers should stay home. In Vesterman,
> pp. 69–77.
> Steinem, G. (1972). Sisterhood. In Vesterman, pp. 48–53.
> Vesterman, W. (Ed.). (1991). *Readings for the 21st Century*. Boston:
> Allyn & Bacon.

Note: These entries should be mingled with all others on the reference page in alphabetical order so cross references may appear before or after the primary source. The year cited should be the date when the cited work was published, not when the Vesterman book was published; such information is usually found in a headnote, footnote, or list of credits at the front or back of the anthology. (See another example of cross-referencing in the sample APA paper on page 136.)

Edition

Cite all editions except the first.

> Campbell, N. A., & Reece, J. B. (2001). *Biology* (6th ed.). New York:
> Pearson Education.

Editor or Compiler

Place "(Ed.)" or "(Eds.)" after the name of the editor(s) and before the date:

> Ghosh, R., & Ray, D. (Eds.). (1995). *Social change and education in
> Canada* (3rd ed.). Toronto: Harcourt Brace.

Encyclopedias, Dictionaries, and Other Alphabetized Reference Books

> Corelli, R. (1999). How are Canadians different from Americans?
> *The Canadian Encyclopedia*. Toronto: McLelland & Stewart.

10d

Kiosk: Word history. (1992). In *The American heritage dictionary of the American language* (3rd ed., p. 993). Boston: Houghton Mifflin.

Note: Give the volume number for multi-volume works (Vol. 4, pp. 19–20).

Bibliography Form—Periodicals

For journal or magazine articles, use the following order. Items 1, 2, 3, 7, and 8 are required.

1. Author
2. Title of the article
3. Name of the periodical
4. Series number (if it is relevant)
5. Volume number (for journals)
6. Issue number (if needed)
7. Date of publication
8. Page numbers

Abstract of a Published Article

Misumi, J., & Fujita, M. (1982). Effects of PM organizational development in supermarket organization. *Japanese Journal of Experimental Social Psychology, 21,* 93–111. Abstract obtained from *Psychological Abstracts,* 1982, *68,* Abstract No. 11474.

Abstract of an Unpublished Work

Brownridge, D. A. (2000). The etiology of male partner violence against women in common-law and marital unions: An analysis of a national survey in Canada. Abstract of unpublished doctoral dissertation, University of Manitoba. (UMI-ProQuest Digital Dissertations, Abstract No. AAT NQ51631).

Abstract Retrieved from InfoTrac, Silverplatter, ProQuest, or Other Servers

Rapin, I. (1997). Autism [rev. of article]. *The New England Journal of Medicine, 337,* 97–104. Abstract retrieved August 4, 1997, from *Expanded Academic Index,* Abstract No. A19615909.

Note: Do not quote from the abstract unless the server stipulates that the author wrote the abstract.

Article in a Journal

Zboril-Benson, L. R. (2002). Why nurses are calling in sick: The impact of health-care restructuring. *Journal of Nursing Research 33(4),* 89–108.

Include the issue number if each issue is paged anew.

Article in a Journal, Two to Six Authors

Johnson, E. A., & Stewart, D. W. (2000). Clinical supervision in
Canadian academic and service settings: The importance of
education, training, and workplace support for supervisor
development. *Canadian Psychology, 41,* 124–130.

Follow the same guidelines outlined above for books, giving surnames and
initials for up to six authors, and using "et al.," for seven or more authors.

Article in a Magazine

Deacon, J. (2001, March 26). Rink rage. *Maclean's, 114,* 13.

Article in a Newspaper

Devlin, K. (1997, August 8). "Soft" mathematics can help us
understand the human mind. *Chronicle of Higher Education,*
pp. B4–B5.

Review

Daneman, M. (2001). [Review of the book *Converging methods for
understanding reading and dyslexia*]. *Canadian Psychology,
42,* 143–145.

Jones, S. L. (1991). The power of motivation [Review of the motion
picture *Body Heat*]. *Contemporary Film Review, 31,* 18.

Report

The Bureau of Tobacco Control. (1999). *Report on Tobacco Control.*
Ottawa: Health Canada.

Bibliography Form—Non-Print Material

Corborn, W. H. (1990, November 3). On facing the fears caused by
nightmares [Interview]. Lexington, KY.

Tabata, S. (Producer). (1998). *Transitions to postsecondary
learning: Video and instructional material for students with
learning disabilities and/or attention deficit disorder*
[Videotape]. Vancouver: Eaton Coull Learning Group.

10d

Bibliography Form—Electronic Sources

When citing Internet sources, include page numbers only if you have that data
from a printed version of the journal or magazine. If the periodical has no
volume number, use "p." or "pp." before the numbers; if the journal has a
volume number, omit "p." or "pp." End the entry with the word "Retrieved"
followed by the date of access and the URL. (URLs can be quite long, but you
must provide the full data for other researchers to find the source.)

Abstract

Bowman, M. L. (2000). The diversity of diversity: Canadian-
American differences and their implications for clinical

training and APA accreditation. [Abstract]. *Canadian Psychology, 41.4*. Retrieved March 30, 2002, from www.cpa.ca/cp/tc-cpnov00.html

Article from an Online Journal

Dow, J. (2000). External and internal approaches to emotion: Commentary on Nesse on mood. *Psycoloquy*. Retrieved September 23, 2000, from www.cogsci.soton.ac.uk/cgi/psyc/newpsy?3.01

Article from a Printed Journal, Reproduced Online

Bowler, D. M., & Thommen, E. (2000). Attribution of mechanical and social causality to animated displays by children with autism. [Electronic version]. *Autism, 4,* 147–172.

Note: Add the URL and date of access if page numbers are not indicated.

Article from a Printed Magazine, Reproduced Online

Vincent, M. (2001, January/February). Canadians at home, work and play in 1900, 1950 and 2001. *Canadian Geographic*. Retrieved June 26, 2001, from http://www.cangeo.ca/

Article from an Online Magazine, No Author Listed

Health-care inflation: It's baaack! (1997, March 17). *Business Week,* 56–62. Retrieved March 18, 1997, from http://www.businessweek.com/1997/11/b351852.html

Article from an Online Newspaper

Kennedy, M. (2001, April 9). Ottawa to set up national organ donor program. *National Post Online*. Retrieved April 27, 2001, from http://www.nationalpost.com/

Bulletins and Government Documents

Canadian Pharmacists Association. (1998). *Herbal and homeopathic products: Ensuring safe choices for Canadians: Report of the advisory panel on herbal remedies.* Retrieved June 28, 2001, from http://www.cdnpharm.ca/cphanew/nv/herbrief.htm

Canada. Parliament. House of Commons. (1999, October 14). *Youth Criminal Justice Act*, Bill C-3, First Reading (36th Parliament, 2nd Session). Retrieved September 19, 2001, from www.parl.gc.ca/36/2/parlbus/chambus/house/bills/government/C-3/C-3_1/C-3TOCE.html

Listserv (E-mail Discussion Group)

Fitzpatrick, B. T. (2000, November 5). Narrative bibliography. Message posted to e-mail: bryanfitzpatrick@mail.csu.edu

But see also "E-mail," page 122.

10d

News Groups

Haas, H. (2000, August 5). Link checker that works with cold fusion. Fogo archives. Message posted to impressive.net/ archives/fogo/200000805113615.AI4381@w3.org

Review, Online

Ebert, R. (2001, January 5). *Traffic* [Review of the motion picture *Traffic*]. Retrieved April 5, 2001, from www.suntimes.com/ ebert/ebert_reviews/2001/01/010501.html

Bibliography Form—CD-ROM and Aggregated Databases

Material from a CD-ROM requires that you identify the database server or the name of the diskette, as shown in the following examples.

Abstract

Figueredo, A. J., & McCloskey, L. A. (1993). Sex, money, and paternity: The evolutionary psychology of domestic violence. *Ethnology and Sociobiology, 14,* 353–79. Abstract retrieved June 12, 2001, from Silverplatter database.

Encyclopedia Article

Social sciences in Canada (2001). *The Canadian Encyclopedia 2001.* Toronto, ON: McClelland & Stewart. Retrieved Mar 25, 2002, from CD-ROM.

Full-Text Article

Borman, W. C., Hanson, M. A., Oppler, S. H., Pulakos, E. D., & White, L. A. (1993). Role of early supervisory experience in supervisor performance. *Journal of Applied Psychology, 78,* 443–449. Retrieved May 23, 2001, from PsycARTICLES database.

10e   Formatting the Paper in APA Style

10e

Place your materials in this order:

1. Title page
2. Abstract
3. Text of the paper
4. References
5. Appendix (optional)

Title Page

In addition to the title of your paper, your name, and your academic affiliation, the title page should establish the running head that will appear on every page, preceding the page number. The APA style requires a shortened form of the paper's title as the running head. See page 131 for an example of a title page in APA style.

Abstract

You should provide an abstract with every paper written in APA style. An abstract is a quick but thorough summary of the contents of your paper. For theoretical papers, the abstract should include the following:

- The topic in one sentence, if possible.
- The purpose, thesis, and scope of the paper.
- A brief reference to the sources used (e.g., published articles, books, personal observation).
- The conclusions and the implications of the study.

For a report of an empirical study, the abstract should include the four items listed above for theoretical papers with the addition of three more:

- Description of the subjects (e.g., species, number, age, type).
- Description of the methodology, including procedures and apparatus.
- The findings produced by the study.

Text of the Paper

Double-space throughout your entire paper. In general you should use subtitles as side heads and centred heads in your paper. See "Headings" in the Appendix for guidelines on writing headings in your paper.

Follow your instructor's guidelines for formatting your paper (e.g., margins, indentations, use of fonts). Otherwise, prepare your paper as shown in the student example on pages 131–135.

References

Present the entries with a hanging indentation, as shown in 10d, pages 123–129.

Appendix

The appendix is the appropriate place for material that is not germane to your text but nevertheless is pertinent to the study: graphs, charts, study plans, observation and test results.

10f

10f   Sample Paper in APA Style

The following paper demonstrates the format and style of a paper written in APA style, with a title page, a running head, an abstract, in-text citations to name the author and year of each source, and a list of references.

The running head will appear at the top of each page.

Aboriginal Education in Canada:
A Work in Progress

by
C. Turenne

129.181 School and Society
Dr. C. Crippen
21 February 2001

10f

Abstract

Place the
abstract
separately on
page 2.

Do not use a
paragraph
indentation for
the abstract.

The abstract
should not
exceed 120
words.

To develop an education system which reflects their cultural and spiritual values, yet remains compatible with provincial systems and post-secondary institutions, Aboriginal people must not only set educational goals but also redefine their relationship to the federal government. In 1972, the residential school system (described as both "cultural genocide" and "internal colonialism") was replaced by band- and community-controlled education, but this "control" was affected by lack of funding, poorly constructed schools, and a shortage of trained Aboriginal teachers. Aboriginals must now take their educational destinies into their own hands, determining their educational direction and promoting decolonization. The way they handle this empowerment and the non-Aboriginal societal response will significantly affect the evolution of this educational work in progress.

10f

As the Aboriginal people of Canada can confirm, colonization is an infantilizing process, taking a vigorous culture and forcing it into a childlike dependency on another (Perley, 1993). In 1972, however, with *Indian Control of Indian Education (ICIE)*, a policy paper from the National Indian Brotherhood, Aboriginal people emerged from that "childhood" into a kind of "adolescence" by declaring their right to determine their identities, their futures, and their relationship to the rest of Canada. This metaphorical adolescence, as with any adolescence, is a difficult period of choices and tensions for Aboriginals, as they not only set educational goals, but also redefine their relationship to the authority figure (in this case, the federal government).

Through experiential learning, Aboriginal children had always been taught the particular skills needed in the environment that would support them (Kirkness, 1992). However, the arrival of the European settlers and the establishment of the residential school system disrupted and contradicted this process entirely. Mercredi (1999) noted that "residential schools are the most common experience for contemporary aboriginal adults." Because of the expressed design of eradicating the language and customs of the First Nations of Canada, the character of Aboriginal education thereafter has been described as "cultural genocide" (Chrisjohn & Young, 1997; Pauls, 1996), and as "internal colonialism" (Perley, 1993, p. 129).

In an attempt to end this situation, in 1969 the federal government proposed that Aboriginal children should no longer be treated as wards of the state but instead as citizens of the provinces in which they lived. Aboriginals' rejection of this proposal (because it was not the government's place to direct that change, whether or not it would be beneficial) was formalized in the policy paper, *Indian Control of Indian Education* (National Indian Brotherhood, 1972). Hereafter, control of Aboriginal education began to devolve to local bands and communities.

Cite the year immediately after the name of the source.

Do not cite a page number for Internet sites; see page 127.

Use & in citations, but not in the text.

10f

Aboriginal 4

[A portion of this paper has been omitted]

Aboriginals, in short, have to take their destinies into their own hands. What they will do with their empowerment, though, is where the challenge lies. Essentially the goals of education are to prepare children to acquire life skills and promote a sense of cultural identity (Charleston, 1988). Many, including Archibald (1995), argued that curricula should reflect the learners' heritage and be created with local Aboriginal people. However, all parties acknowledge the importance of an education system that is compatible with both provincial or territorial systems, and with post-secondary institutions (Charleston, 1988). How educators balance compatibility and uniqueness seems a daunting task.

[A portion of this paper has been omitted]

Several questions remain: How do educators design a Native education that does not just assimilate or undermine Aboriginal values and customs? How will Native cultures adapt and create curricula that embrace the reality of diverse populations, without unwittingly abandoning their children outside the reach of such curricula? Unfortunately, the literature provides few answers, although LaFrance (2000), Watt-Cloutier (2000), and Williams (2000) have described several innovative projects in Akwesasne (ON), Nunavik (QC), and Vancouver (BC), respectively. These programs affirmed that Aboriginal education is growing, strengthening, and maturing. Education is the most significant function a society can perform, and all societies have developed it according to their needs and interests. Castellano, Davis, and Lahache (2000) stressed:

> The old story is one of destruction and pain, while the emerging one is that of the ongoing vitality of Aboriginal people, from whose experience we can learn. Aboriginal people believe that education is an integral way of helping the new story unfold. (p. ix)

10f

Use the past tense or present perfect tense when citing sources.

Indent long quotations of 40 words or more five additional spaces, and omit the quotation marks.

   Naturally, given the human condition of imperfection, mistakes will be made. However, it is the unnatural relationship of colonialism that makes non-Natives think that they have the right or responsibility to "prevent" mistakes and that Aboriginals have to "accept" this wisdom. Throughout this work in progress, as the planning of Aboriginal education develops and matures, the societal response of non-Aboriginal people must also develop and mature.

10f

References

Book

Alladin, M. I. (Ed.). (1996). *Racism in Canadian Schools*. Toronto: Harcourt Brace.

Archibald, J. (1995). To keep the fire going: The challenge for First Nations education in the year 2000. In Ghosh & Ray, pp. 342–357.

Primary reference to an anthology

Castellano, M. B., Davis, L., & Lahache, L. (Eds.). (2000). *Aboriginal education: Fulfilling the promise*. Vancouver: UBC Press.

Charleston, M. (Ed.) (1988). Quality of First Nations education. In National Indian Brotherhood, Assembly of First Nations, *Tradition and education: Towards a vision of our future* (pp. 71–83). Summerstown, ON: Author.

Chrisjohn, R., & Young, S. (1997). *The circle game: Shadows and substances in the Indian residential school experience in Canada*. Penticton: Theytus. Also available in *For seven generations: An information legacy of the Royal Commission on Aboriginal Peoples*. [CD-ROM]. Ottawa: Libraxus.

Ghosh, R., & Ray, D. (Eds.). (1995). *Social change and education in Canada*. Toronto: Harcourt Brace.

Kirkness, V. J. (1992). *First Nations and schools: Triumphs and struggles*. Toronto: Canadian Education Association.

Cross reference to the primary source (Castellano, Davis, & Lahache)

Lafrance, B. T. (1993). Culturally negotiated education in First Nations communities: Empowering ourselves for future generations. In Castellano, Davis, & Lahache, pp. 101–113.

Internet source

Mercredi, O. (1999, March). Aboriginal education: Ovide Mercredi reflects. *Professionally Speaking*. Retrieved January 15, 2001, from www.oct.on.ca/english/ps/march_1999/ovide.htm

National Indian Brotherhood. (1972). *Indian control of Indian education*. Policy paper presented to the Minister of Indian Affairs and Northern Development. Ottawa: Author.

Pauls, S. (1996). Racism and Native schooling: A historical perspective. In Alladin, pp. 22–41.

10f

Perley, D. G. (1993). Aboriginal education in Canada as internal colonialism. *Canadian Journal of Native Education 20,* 128–138.

Watt-Cloutier, S. (1993). Honouring our past, creating our future: Education in northern and remote communities. In Castellano, Davis, and Lahache, pp. 114–128.

Williams, L. (1994). Urban Aboriginal education: The Vancouver experience. In Castellano, Davis, & Lahache, pp. 129–146.

Journal article

10f

11 Using the CBE Styles for Scientific Papers

The Council of Biology Editors, now known as the Council of Science Editors, established two separate forms for citing sources in scientific writing. One CBE style is the **citation-sequence** system for writing in the applied sciences, such as chemistry, computer science, mathematics, physics, and medicine. It uses a number in the text to represent each source.

> The original description (3) contained precise taxonomic detail that differed with recent studies (4–6).

The other CBE style is the **name-year** system for use in the biological and earth sciences.

> The original description (Roberts 1999) contained precise taxonomic detail that differed with recent studies (McCormick 2000a, 2000b, and Tyson and others 1999).

There are advantages and disadvantages to each system. The citation-sequence system saves space, and the numbers make minimal disruption to the reading of the text. The name-year system mentions authors' names in the text with the year to show timely application and historical perspective. In truth, the decision is usually not yours to make. Although there may be exceptions to the following guidelines, the individual disciplines in the sciences have generally adopted one form or the other, as shown in the following chart.

Disciplines Using Citation-Sequence Numbers

Bio-medical Science	Engineering	Medicine
Chemistry	Health	Nursing
Computer Science	Mathematics	Physics

Disciplines Using Name and Year

Agriculture	Astronomy	Geography
Anthropology	Biology	Geology
Archaeology	Botany	Zoology

11a Blending Sources into Your Writing

Writing the In-Text Citations with a Number

The citation-sequence system features numbers in the text to identify the sources, and a list of "Cited References" that are numbered to correspond to the in-text citations.

Assign a number to each entry. One method is to arrange references in alphabetical order and then number them consecutively, in which case the numbers will appear in random order in the text. Another method is to number the references consecutively as you put them into your text, interrupting that order when repeating references cited earlier.

Place the number within parentheses or brackets or as a superscript numeral. Each style is shown in the examples that follow.

Note: A name may be cited in the text but is not required.

> It is known (1) that the DNA concentration of a nucleus doubles during interphase.

> A recent study [1] has raised interesting questions related to photosynthesis, some of which have been answered [2].

> In particular, a recent study[1] has raised many interesting questions related to photosynthesis, some of which have been answered.[2]

If you use the authority's name, add the number after the name.

> Additional testing by Cooper (3) includes alterations in carbohydrate metabolism and changes in ascorbic acid incorporation into the cell and adjoining membranes.

If necessary, add specific data to the entry.

> The results of the respiration experiment published by Jones (3, Table 6, p 412) had been predicted earlier by Smith (5, Proposition 8).

Writing the In-Text Citation with a Name and Year

When writing research papers in accordance with the CBE name-year system, place the year within parentheses immediately after the authority's name.

> Smith (1999) ascribes no species-specific behaviour to man. However, Adams (2000) presents data that tend to be contradictory.

If you do not mention the authority's name in your text, insert the name, year, and even page numbers within the parentheses.

> One source found some supporting evidence for a portion of the questionable data (Marson and Brown 2000, pp 23–32) through point bi-serial correlation techniques.

Unlike APA style, the CBE style does not use the ampersand ("&"). Also, "p" and "pp" are not followed by a period.

For three or more authors, use the lead author's name with "and others."

Note: The CBE style prefers English terms and English abbreviations rather than Latin words and abbreviations such as "et al."

> Torgerson and others (2000)

Use lowercase letters (a, b, c) to identify two or more works published in the same year by the same author: "Thompson (2001a)" and "Thompson (2001b)." If necessary, supply additional information:

11a

Horton (2000a, 2000b; cf. Thomas, 1999, p 89) suggests an intercorrelation of these testing devices. But after multiple-group analysis, Welston (1999, esp. p 211) reached an opposite conclusion.

Using a Quotation or Paraphrase

Jones (1994) found that "these data of psychological development suggest that one class of adolescents is atypical in maturational growth" (p 215).

A long quotation is indented as a block (and therefore omits quotation marks).

Albert (1994) found the following:
> Whenever these pathogenic organisms attack the human body and begin to multiply, the infection is set in motion. The host responds to this parasitic invasion with efforts to cleanse itself of the invading agents. When rejection efforts of the host become visible (fever, sneezing, congestion), the disease status exists (pp 314–315).

Punctuation

Use a comma followed by a space to separate citations of different references by the same author.

Supplemental studies (Johnson 1999a, 1999b, 2000) have shown . . .

Use a comma followed by a space to separate author names accompanied by initials in citations with two or more authors.

(Roberts SL, Rudolph CB, and others 1999)

Use a semicolon followed by a space to separate citations to different authors.

Supplemental studies (Smith, 1999; Barfield 1989, 1997; Barfield and Smith 1998; Wallace 2000) have shown . . .

11b Formatting the Cited References Entries

Supply a Cited References section at the end of your paper. Again, two styles exist. Choose the one appropriate for your paper. If you number the in-text citations, number the reference entries. If you cite name and year in your text, alphabetize the list and do not use numbers.

11b

Citation-Sequence Entries

Each entry in the list should be numbered to correspond to the sources as noted in the text. The examples that follow show the capitalization, punctuation, spacing, and other style elements to use for entries in the Cited References section of your paper.

Book

List the author, title of the book, place of publication, publisher, year, and total number of pages (optional). Do not underline or italicize the title of a book or the title of an article in a book.

1. Gehling E. The family and friends' guide to diabetes: Everything you need to know. New York: Wiley; 2000.

Article in a Journal

Provide the author, the title of the article, the name of the journal, the year and month if necessary, volume number and issue number if listed, and inclusive pages. Do not use quotation marks around article titles and do not underline or italicize journal titles.

2. Bolli GB, Owens DR. Insulin glargine. Lancet 2000;356:443–444.
3. Brancati FL, Kao WHL, Folsom AR, Watson RL, Szklo M. Incident type 2 diabetes mellitus in African American and white adults. JAMA 2000;283:2253–2259.

Internet Articles and Other Electronic Publications

Add the URL for the article as well as the date you accessed the material. Follow the example in number 4 for an article published on the Web. Follow the example in number 5 for a periodical article that has been reproduced on the Web. Number 4 is online and number 5 is a printed journal [serial online].

4. [Anonymous]. Diabetes insipidus. Amer. Acad. of Family Physicians [online] 2000. Available from www.aafp.org/patientinfo/insipidu.html. Accessed 2000 Aug 8.
5. Roberts S. The diabetes advisor. Diabetes Forecast [serial online] 2000;53:41–42. Available from www.diabetes.org/diabetesforecast/00August/default.asp. Accessed 2000 Aug 8.

Magazine and Newspaper Articles

Add a specific date and, for newspapers, cite a section letter or number.

6. Schlosberg S. The symptoms you should never ignore. Shape 2000 Aug:136.
7. [Anonymous]. FDA approval of drug gives diabetics a new choice. Los Angeles Times 2000 Aug 2;Sect A:4.

Proceedings and Conference Presentations

Give the name of the author or editor, the title of the presentation, name of the conference, type of work (report, proceedings, proceedings online, etc.), name of the organization or society, the date of the conference, and the location. If found on the Internet, add the URL and the date you accessed the information.

11b

8. Ashraf H, Banz W, Sundberg J. Soyful luncheon: Setting a healthful table for the community [abstract]. In: Crossing borders: Food and agriculture in the Americas. Proceedings online of the Assn. for the Study of Food and Society; 1999 June 3–6; Toronto (ON). Available from www.acs.ryerson.ca/foodsec/foodsec/papers.html. Accessed 2000 Aug 8.

Article from a Loose-leaf Collection

9. [Anonymous]. No-till farming shows skeptics the advantages of giving up the plow. CQ Researcher 1994;4:1066.

Name-Year Entries

Alphabetize the list and label it "References," "Cited References," or "Literature Cited." Double-space the entries and use the hanging indentation. When there are two to 10 authors, all should be named in the reference listing. When there are 11 or more authors, the first 10 are listed, followed by "and others." If the author is anonymous, insert "[Anonymous]." Place the year immediately after the author's name.

Book

List the author, year, title, place of publication, publisher, and total number of pages (optional).

> Gershuny G, Smillie J. 1999. The soul of soil: A soil-building guide for master gardeners and farmers. White River Junction, Vt.: Chelsea Green. 173 p.

Article in a Journal

List the author, year, article title, journal title, volume number, and inclusive pages. Add an issue number for any journal that is paged anew with each issue.

> Lyons-Johnson D. 1998. Deep-rooted safflower cuts fertilizer losses. Ag. Research 46:17.

Internet Articles and Other Electronic Publications

Add an availability statement as well as the date you accessed the material.

> Ramsel RE, Nelson LA, Wicks GA. 1999. Ecofarming: No-till ecofallow proso millet in winter wheat stubble. NebGuide [online]. Available from www.ianr.unl.edu/pubs/FieldCrops/g835.htm. Accessed 2000 Aug 8.
>
> Barbieri PA, Rozas HR, Andrade FH, Echeverria, HE. 2000. Row spacing effects at different levels of nitrogen availability in maize [abstract]. Agron. J.[serial online];92: 283–287. Available from http://link.springer-ny.com/link/service/journals/10087/bibs/0092002/00920283.html. Accessed 2000 Aug 8.

11b

Magazine and Newspaper Articles

Add a specific date and, if listed, a section letter or number.

> Haag E. 1997 March. Farewell to fallow. Farm Journal 121:E–4.
> Cowen RC. 1996 June 11. No-till farming can reduce nitrogen pollution. Christian Science Monitor 88:14.

Proceedings and Conference Publications

Give author, date, title of the presentation, name of conference, type of work (report, proceeding, proceedings online, etc.), name of the organization or society, and place of the conference. If found on the Internet, add the URL and the date of your access.

> Ashraf H, Banz W, Sundberg J. 1999 June 3–6. Soyful luncheon: Setting a healthful table for the community [abstract]. In: Crossing borders: Food and agriculture in the Americas. [Proceedings online of the Association for the Study of Food and Society]; Toronto (ON). Available from www.acs.ryerson.ca/~foodsec/foodsec/Papers.html. Accessed 2000 Aug 8.

Article from a Loose-leaf Collection

> [Anonymous]. 1994. No-till farming shows skeptics the advantages of giving up the plow. CQ Researcher 4:1066.

11c Arranging the Cited References List

Citation-Sequence Style

Double-space the list of references. Set the numbers flush left. Use your tab key to set the lines of text in a uniform pattern, as shown in the examples.

Numbering the List by the Order of Your In-Text Citations

If you number the in-text citations as you enter them in your manuscript, your Cited References should be numbered without an alphabetical order.

Cited References

1. Cowen RC. 1996 June 11. No-till farming can reduce nitrogen pollution. Christian Science Monitor 88:14.
2. Haag E. 1997 March. Farewell to fallow. Farm Journal 121:E–4.
3. Gershuny G, Smillie J. 1999. The soul of soil: A soil-building guide for master gardeners and farmers. White River Junction, Vt.: Chelsea Green. 173 p.
4. Lyons-Johnson D. 1998. Deep-rooted safflower cuts fertilizer losses. Ag. Research 46:17.
5. Barbieri PA, Rozas HR, Andrade FH, Echeverria, HE. 2000. Row spacing effects at different levels of nitrogen availability in maize [abstract]. Agron. J. [serial online];92:283–287. Available from http://link.springer-ny.com/link/service/journals/10087/bibs/0092002/00920283.html. Accessed 2000 Aug 8.

Numbering the List by Alphabetical Order

You may choose to alphabetize your sources, number them, and use those numbers in your text. If so, your Cited References should look like the list immediately above, but the entries will be in alphabetical order, not the order in which they appear in the text.

Name-Year Style

If you use the name and year system in your text, you should place the Cited References entries in alphabetical order, as shown next. Do not number the list, and use the hanging indentation shown here.

11c

Cited References

Barbieri PA, Rozas HR, Andrade FH, Echeverria, HE. 2000. Row spacing effects at different levels of nitrogen availability in maize [abstract]. Agron. J. [serial online];92:283–287. Available from http://link.springer-ny.com/link/service/journals/10087/bibs/0092002/00920283.html. Accessed 2000 Aug 8.

Cowen RC. 1996 June 11. No-till farming can reduce nitrogen pollution. Christian Science Monitor 88:14.

Gershuny G, Smillie J. 1999. The soul of soil: A soil-building guide for master gardeners and farmers. White River Junction, Vt.: Chelsea Green. 173 p.

Haag E. 1997 March. Farewell to fallow. Farm Journal 121:E–4.

Lyons-Johnson D. 1998. Deep-rooted safflower cuts fertilizer losses. Ag. Research 46:17.

11d Sample Paper Using the CBE Citation-Sequence Number System

The paper that follows demonstrates the format for a paper using the CBE citation-sequence number system, with superscript numbers ([1]). However, your instructor may require you to use numbers within parentheses (1) or brackets [1] instead. Most instructors will also require headings, an abstract (see APA style page 130), and running heads.

Do not number the title page, but consider it page 1. The running head will start on page 2.

11d

Canadian Regulation of Herbal Remedies

Jennifer Kroetsch

99.111 Introduction to the University
Professor B. Rudyk
November 25, 2001

Introduction

In the 21st century, most North Americans do not use folk remedies involving lemons cut in the form of a cross and applied to the head to cure headaches.[1] Yet when illness becomes personal or affects a loved one, people often try any avenue to be cured. In many cases, this route leads to herbal remedies or Natural Health Products (NHPs).[2,3,4] It has been reported that the number of Canadians using herbal remedies doubled from 15% in 1996 to 30% in 1998,[4] and that the worldwide herbal industry is currently estimated at more than 10 billion dollars.[5] However, health professionals caution that herbal remedies should be used judiciously since defining and regulating these potentially dangerous products is problematic.

Sources are numbered in the order in which they are mentioned in the text. More than one source can be listed for one idea or concept.

Discussion

It might seem that the best source of information regarding NHPs is a physician. However, physicians have long been frustrated by the lack of reliable information on herbal remedies.[6] Since it has been technically difficult to detect many of the side effects of herbal plants, there is little scientific information on NHPs available even to health professionals.[7] Recently, however, in collaboration with the Canadian Pharmacists' Association, the Canadian Medical Association (CMA) published the book entitled Herbs: Everyday Resource for Health Professionals, which has been received enthusiastically by physicians.[8]

Headings are usually used in CBE style.

Because the trend towards alternative medicine is so strong, more and more people are buying products with the words "herbal" or "natural" on the label and, surprisingly, the label can be the most deceiving source.[9] It has been claimed that the chance of the information on the label being accurate is about 30%.[4] Thadani explained that if the producing company makes no medical claims on the label, these products can be sold

11d

Use original number assigned to reference when citing it again.

as food rather than as drugs,[10] thus exempting NHPs from the regulations applied to drugs. A 1999 survey of the use of, and attitudes to, alternative medicine in Canada revealed that close to 90% of Canadians are lobbying the government to exert pressure on manufacturers to provide more information on the active ingredients and side effects of their herbal products.[11]

In response to these public demands, a new regulatory organization—the Office of Natural Health Products (ONHP)—was created by the federal government in 1999,[4] and in July 2000 this office was upgraded to a full directorate.[11] As well, the CMA is consulting with the ONHP regarding a proposed regulatory framework for NHPs.

The ONHP claims that the greatest challenge for this new office will be to define health products, noting that since Canada is the first country to attempt to regulate NHPs, other countries are appraising with acute interest the success of this trial. [4]

[A portion of this paper has been omitted]

The federal government's efforts to define and regulate NHPs is an encouraging response to demands from the public and from the CMA for a regulatory framework for herbal remedies. However, in view of the lack of current research, consumers must treat NHPs as cautiously as they would treat any prescription drug, evaluating carefully the chances of unwanted side effects. Canadians are exhibiting an increasing need to participate actively in their health care; they can, in part, satisfy this desire by evaluating the safety and quality of NHPs and by continuing to lobby for the regulation of herbal remedies.

11d

Herbal Remedies 4

References

1. Pollak-Eltz A. Folk medicine in Venezuela. Fohrenau: Medieninhaber, Verleger and Hersteller; 1982. 503 p.
2. Kozyrskyj A. Herbal products in Canada. Can Family Physician 1997;43:697–702.
3. Eisenberg DM. Advising patients who seek medical therapies. Annals of Internal Medicine. 1997;127:61–9.
4. Sibbald B. New federal office will spend millions to regulate herbal remedies, vitamins. CMAJ [online] 1999 May 4;160:1355-7. www.cma.ca/cmaj/ vol-160/issue-9/1355.htm. Accessed 2001 Apr 5.
5. Manitoba Agriculture and Food. Herb and spice industry overview. [online] 2001 Jun 4. www. gov.mb.ca/agriculture/financial/agribus/ ccg02s00.html. Accessed 2001 Jun 27.
6. Thompson CA. As patients embrace herbal remedies, dearth of scientific evidence frustrates clinicians. Amer J of Health-System Pharm. 1997;54:2656–8, 2664.
7. Hoffmann D, editor. The information sourcebook of herbal medicine. Freedom (CA): Crossing Press; 1994.
8. Canadian Medical Association. Groundbreaking new book on herbal remedies created by CMA and the Canadian Pharmacists Association. [online] 2000 Apr 17. www.cma.ca/advocacy/news/ 2000/04-17.htm. Accessed 2001 Apr 25.
9. Greenwald J. Herbal healing. Time 1998 Nov 23: 47–57.

The numbers correspond to the order in which the sources were mentioned in the text.

The total number of pages in a *book* is sometimes added at the end of the reference.

11d

10. Thadani M. Herbal remedies: Weeding fact from fiction. Winnipeg (MB): Cantext; 1999.
11. Canadian Medical Association. Natural health products: ensuring safety, quality and efficacy. [online] 2000 Sep 29. www.cma.ca/advocacy/political/2000/09-29.htm. Accessed 2001 Apr 25.

11d

12 Using the CMS (Chicago) Note Style

The fine arts and some fields in the humanities, but not literature, employ traditional footnotes or endnotes, which should conform to standards set by *The Chicago Manual of Style,* 14th edition, 1993.

12a   Blending Sources into Your Writing

With this system, you must employ superscript numerals within the text (like this[15]) and place documentary notes either as footnotes on corresponding pages or as endnotes that appear together at the end of the paper.

Although a "Bibliography" page (the equivalent of the "Works Cited" or "Sources Cited" page in MLA and the "References" page in APA and CBE) is not always required in CMA, some instructors may ask for one at the end of the paper. If so, see the examples on page 155 and in the "Works Cited" at the end of the sample paper, on page 162. This page may be entitled "Selected Bibliography," "Works Cited," or "Sources Cited." Consult your instructor about the preferred title. Running heads and an abstract are optional in this style.

The following discussion assumes that notes will appear as footnotes. However, some instructors accept endnotes; that is, all notes appear together at the end of the paper, not at the bottom of individual pages. (See page 154).

If available, use the footnote or endnote feature of your software. It will not only insert the raised superscript numeral but also keep your footnotes arranged properly at the bottom of each page. In most instances, the software will first insert the superscript numeral and then skip to the bottom of the page so you can write the footnote. It will not, of course, write the note automatically; you must type in the essential data in the correct style.

It is customary to write in the present tense when using the Chicago footnote style.

Writing with Superscript Numerals in the Text

Use Arabic numerals typed slightly above the line (like this[12]). Place this superscript numeral at the end of quotations or paraphrases, with the numeral following without a space after the final word or mark of punctuation, as in this sample:

> Under Louis XIV the church in Canada became subordinate to the
> needs and dictates of the state. The crown determined the number of

clergy, defined their roles in the colony, and provided up to 40 percent of the church's revenue.[18] The church's main role was to ensure the subordination of colonists to spiritual and secular authority.[19] The church "attempted to cultivate an ethic of obligation and obedience, of simplicity and austerity."[20]

The superscript numerals go outside the marks of punctuation. Avoid placing one superscript numeral at the end of a long paragraph because readers will not know if it refers to only the final sentence or to the entire paragraph. If you introduce borrowed materials with an authority's name and then place a superscript numeral at the end, you direct the reader to the full extent of the borrowed material.

Kirkness notes that before the Europeans arrived, education in Aboriginal society was already evolved: every adult had the responsibility to ensure that every child learned "how to live a good life."[1] Kirkness adds, "Not only was education geared to teaching the values of the society, but also its economics."[2]

An advantage of the Chicago footnote style is that, unlike MLA or APA, you can include content or explanatory notes (see 12e).

12b   Formatting the Notes in CMS Style

Place your footnotes at the bottom of pages to correspond with superscript numerals (see immediately above). Whether you directly quote, paraphrase, or use the ideas of your source, you must credit each source in a footnote with a page number. Note that "p" and "pp" are not used in footnotes or endnotes. Some papers will require footnotes on almost every page. Follow these conventions:

1. **Spacing and indention.** Single space individual footnotes, but double space between footnotes. Indent the first line five spaces, as you would a normal paragraph.
2. **Numbering.** Number the notes consecutively throughout the entire paper. The raised superscript numeral is preferred if your computer software provides it.
3. **Placement.** Collect at the bottom of each page all footnotes to citations made on that page.
4. **Distinguish footnotes from text.** Separate footnotes from the text by triple spacing. See the sample paper, pages 156–162.

Writing Notes for Books

Begin with the footnote number, followed by a period and a space, if the number is typed on the line. If you use a superscript numeral, it is *not* followed by a period or a space. Both methods are demonstrated in the following examples citing books. For the rest of the examples, superscript numerals are used. Follow the number with the name of the author in regular order, that is, first name followed by last name, followed by a comma; the title (italicized or underlined); the publication information (place, publisher, and year within parentheses); and a page reference.

12b

Book, One to Three Authors

[1]Orest Martynowych, *Ukrainians in Canada: The Formative Period, 1891–1924* (Edmonton: Canadian Institute of Ukrainian Studies Press, 1991), 25.

2. Marilyn J. Boxer and Jean H. Quataert, eds., *Connecting Spheres: European Women in a Globalizing World, 1500 to the Present,* 2nd ed. (New York: Oxford University Press, 2000), chap. 2, esp. 33.

Book, More Than Three Authors

[3]Alison Prentice et al., *Canadian Women: A History.* 2nd ed. (Toronto: Harcourt Brace Canada, 1996), 531.

Book, Part of an Anthology or Collection

[4]Barry Came, "The Red River Flood, Spring, 1997," in *In the Face of Disaster: True Stories of Canadian Heroism from the Archives of Maclean's.* ed. Michael Benedict (Toronto: Viking, 2000), 71.

[5]George Hersey, "Female and Male Art: *Postille* to Garrard's *Artemisia Gentileschi,*" in *Parthenope's Splendour: Art of the Golden Age in Naples,* ed. Jeanne Porter and Susan Munshower (University Park, PA: Pennsylvania State University Press, 1993), 325.

Writing Notes for Periodicals

Article from a Journal

[6]Herb Enns, "Achieving the Modern: Abstract Painting and Design in the 1950's," *Canadian Architect* 38 (1993): 26.

Article from a Magazine

[7]Ken MacQueen, "Wild Woman of the West: Who Were You, Emily Carr?" *Maclean's,* 11 June 2001, 62.

Article from a Newspaper

[8]Peter Crossley, "Leathers on Art Buying," *Winnipeg Free Press,* 4 November 1967, A11.

Review Article

[9]Griselda Pollock, review of *Artemisia Gentileschi: The Image of the Female Hero in Italian Baroque Art,* by Mary Garrard, *Art Bulletin,* 15 March 1994, 505.

Writing Notes for Electronic Sources

The Chicago Manual of Style (CMS) uses brackets to describe the type of electronic source, shows when it was first cited, published, or accessed, and gives an electronic address. The CMS does not supply a great deal of information on citing electronic sources, but the University of Chicago Press suggests consulting *Online! A Reference Guide to Using Internet Sources* by Harnack and

12b

Kleppinger (available in print and online at **www.bedfordstmartins.com/ online/cite7.html**) which contains a chapter entitled "Using Chicago Style to Cite and Document Sources."

Article from an Online Journal

[10]Gao Yi; "French Revolutionary Studies in Today's China," *Canadian Journal of History* 32 (1997), <www.usask.ca/history/cjh/> (19 June 2001).

Article from an Online Magazine

[11]Robert Smith, "Escape from Culloden," *British Heritage*, February/March 2001, <www.thehistorynet.com/BritishHeritage/ articles/2001/02012_cover.htm> (20 April 2001).

Book Online

[12] D. H. Lawrence, *Lady Chatterly's Lover,* 1928, <http://bibliomania.com/fiction/dhl/chat.html> (16 May 2001).

CD-ROM Source

[13]Aurelio J. Figueredo and Laura Ann McCloskey, "Sex, Money, and Paternity: the Evolutionary Psychology of Domestic Violence," *Ethnology and Sociobiology* 14 (1993): 355, PsycLIT [CD-ROM]; available from Silverplatter.

Electronic Bulletin Board

[14]Rosemary Camilleri, "Narrative Bibliography," <listserv@ H-RHETOR@msu.edu> (March 1997).

E-mail

Because e-mail is not retrievable, do not document with a note or bibliography entry. Instead, mention the name of the source within your text by saying something like this:

> Walter Wallace argues that teen violence stems mainly from the breakup of the traditional family (e-mail to the author).

Government Document Online

[15]Canada. House of Commons. Standing Committee on Canadian Heritage. *The Challenge of Change: A Consideration of the Canadian Book Industry*. The Report of the Standing Committee on Canadian Heritage, Ottawa: Public Works and Government Services Canada, 21 June 2000, <www.cmhc-schl.gc.ca/en/index.cfm?pMenu=72> (11 July 2001).

Scholarly Project Online

[16] *British Poetry Archive*, ed. Jerome Mcgann and David Seaman, 1999, <http://etext.lib.virginia.edu/britpo.html> (7 March 2002).

12b

Writing Notes for Other Sources

Biblical Reference

[17]Rom. 6:2.

[17]1 Cor. 13.1–3.

Encyclopedia

[18]*The World Book Encyclopedia*, 2000 ed., s.v. "Raphael."

Note: sub verbo ("s.v.") means "under the word(s)."

Government Documents

[19]Canada. Commission of Inquiry into the Deployment of Canadian Forces to Somalia. *Dishonoured Legacy: The Lessons of the Somalia Affair: Report of the Commission of Inquiry into the Deployment of Canadian Forces to Somalia: Executive Summary,* by Gilles Letourneau. Ottawa: Minister of Public Works and Government Services Canada: Canada Communications Group, 1997.

[20]United Kingdom, *Coroner's Act, 1954*, 2 & 3 Eliz. 2, ch. 31.

Non-print Source: Lecture, Sermon, Speech, Oral Report

[21]JoAnne G. Bernstein, "The Renaissance Nude: Studio Practice and the Modern Gaze," Lecture (University of California, San Diego, 27 April 1994).

Television

[22]Holly Doan, *Frida, Georgia and Emily Carr* (Winnipeg: WTN, 10 June 2001).

Film

[23]*Surviving Picasso*, 35mm, 123 min., Warner Brothers, 1996.

Musical Work

[24]Wolfgang A. Mozart, *Symphony no. 41 in C major, K. 551 "Jupiter,"* The London Classical Players, Roger Norrington, EMI 7 54090 2.

12c Citing Subsequent Footnotes after the First

After a first full reference, subsequent footnotes should be shortened to author's name and page number, for example, "Bumsted, 92." When an author has two works mentioned, employ a shortened version of the title, for example, "Friesen, *River,* 25." In general, avoid Latinate abbreviations such as *loc. cit.* or *op. cit.;* however, whenever a note refers to the source in the immediately preceding note, you may use "Ibid." to refer to the same page number of the preceding entry or use "Ibid." with a new page number as shown in Section 12d below (note especially the differences between notes 2, 7, and 8).

12c

12d Writing a Notes Section for Endnotes

If you are using endnotes rather than footnotes, put all your notes together in a Notes section at the end of your paper. Most computer software programs offer features that help you with this task. The disadvantage of this method is that the reader has to flip back and forth to follow your citations. Follow these conventions:

1. **Form.** Use the form explained earlier in 12b and 12c.
2. **Title.** Begin the notes on a new page at the end of the text. Entitle the page "Notes" centred and placed two inches from the top of the page.
3. **Indention.** Indent the first line of each note five spaces, type the note number in regular Arabic numerals, or use superscript numerals placed slightly above the line. Begin the note and use the left margin for succeeding lines.
4. **Spacing.** Triple space between the heading and the first note. Single space the notes and double space between the notes, as shown in this example of notes from a paper on the women's movement in Canada in the last half of the 20th century.

Notes

[1]Alvin Finkel, Margaret Conrad, and Veronica Strong-Boag, *History of the Canadian Peoples 1867 to the Present* (Toronto: Copp Clark Pitman, 1993), 543.

[2]Ibid., 545.

[3]Barry Came and Bruce Wallace, "The Lepine Massacre, December 6, 1989" in Michael Benedict, ed., *In the Face of Disaster: True Stories of Canadian Heroism from the Archives of Maclean's* (Toronto: Viking, 2000), 160.

[4]Nancy Sheehan, "Sexism in Education" in *Social Change and Education in Canada*, 3rd. ed. Ratna Ghosh and Douglas Ray (Toronto: Harcourt Brace Canada, 1995), 328.

[5]Came and Wallace, 163.

[6]Carol Gilligan, *In a Different Voice* (Boston: Harvard University Press, 1982), 25.

[7]Finkel, Conrad, and Strong-Boag, 545.

[8]Ibid.

[9]Sheehan, 333.

[10]Finkel, Conrad, and Strong-Boag, 555.

12e

12e Writing Content or Explanatory Notes

Use a content endnote to explain research problems, to resolve or report conflicts in the testimony of the critics, to provide interesting tidbits, and to credit people and sources not mentioned in the text. Content or explanatory footnotes should be intermingled with your documented footnotes. Here is an example:

40. There are three copies of the papal brief situated on Via S. Nicola da Tolentino. The document is printed in Thomas D. Culley, *Jesuits and Music* (Rome and St. Louis, 1979), 1: 358–59.

For additional discussion and examples, see the appendix, pages 168–169 and footnote number 2 in the sample paper at the end of this chapter.

12f   Writing a Bibliography Page for a Paper That Uses Footnotes or Endnotes

In addition to footnotes or endnotes, you may need to supply a separate bibliography page that lists sources used in developing the paper. Check with your instructor before preparing one because it may not be required. Use a heading that represents its contents, such as "Selected Bibliography," "Sources Consulted," or "Works Cited."

Separate the title from the first entry with a triple space. Use a hanging indent; type the first line of each entry flush left; indent the second line and other succeeding lines five spaces. Alphabetize the list by last names of authors. Single space the lines of each item, but double space between the items. List alphabetically by title two or more works by one author. The basic forms are as follows:

Book

Finkel, Alvin, Margaret Conrad, and Veronica Strong-Boag, *History of the Canadian Peoples 1867 to the Present*. Toronto: Copp Clark Pitman, 1993.

Schirokauer, Conrad. *A Brief History of Japanese Civilization*. New York: Harcourt, 1993.

Journal Article

Silvers, Annette. "Has Her(oine's) Time Now Come?" *Journal of Aesthetics and Art Criticism* 48 (1990): 365–79.

Newspaper

Fine, Sean. "Aboriginal Languages Face Extinction." *The Globe and Mail*, 20 June 2001.

See also the bibliography page that accompanies the sample paper, page 162.

12g   Sample Paper Using the CMS (Chicago) Footnote System

The following paper demonstrates the correct form for a research paper using the CMS (Chicago) note system. The writer's instructor may have requested that her paper be submitted in MLA style. Consult Chapter 9, pages 112–117 to see how the same paper, "Breaking the Mould" would be written using MLA style.

12g

Breaking the Mould:
Artemisia Gentileschi's Contribution to Art

by
Katrina A. T. Senyk

54.124 Art History
Dr. M. Steggles
March 10, 2002

Most instructors require a title page. The running head (optional in Chicago style) starts on page 2 and will appear at the top of each page.

12g

Senyk 2

Many people believe that artists view the human condition from the unique perspective of their individuality and unconsciously illustrate their perspective via their art, in much the same way that "personality theories are strongly influenced by personal and subjective factors . . . (and) reflect the biographies of their authors."[1] If this is so, then artists' perceptions of the world are translated into their works of art. Moreover, Mary Garrard states that, historically, the "assignment of sex roles has created fundamental differences between the sexes in their perception, experience, and expectations of the world . . . that cannot help but be carried over into the creative process."[2]

Artemisia Gentileschi (1593–c.1652) portrayed her subjects from her unusual perspective as a female artist in the 17th century. Viewers frequently question why Gentileschi painted such powerful female protagonists; by examining Gentileschi's perception of her world, the viewer can better understand what her art represented to her as a woman in a male-dominated profession. Gentileschi's work explores women's demands to be justly represented.

In the 17th century options for women were limited to marrying and raising children, or devotion to the Catholic Church as a nun. Alternatives were not viewed as appropriate. However, Artemisia Gentileschi was more fortunate than her peers; having been born to a painter, she was raised in "an environment where she could

---

[1]B. R. Hergenhahn and Matthew H. Olson, *An Introduction to Theories of Personality,* 5th ed. (Toronto: Prentice Hall Canada, 1999), 569.

[2]Mary Garrard, *Artemisia Gentileschi: The Image of the Female Hero in Italian Baroque Art* (Princeton: Princeton UP, 1989), 202. For a detailed discussion of the heroic image see Garrard's whole work.

Margin annotations:

Katrina identifies the issue and cites sources in her opening to confirm the serious nature of the discussion. See pages 79–81 for details about writing the introduction.

Katrina uses raised superscript numerals.

Katrina expresses her thesis in a sentence at the end of the introduction.

Katrina adds an explanatory note to the Garrard reference (one of the advantages of the footnote system).

12g

Senyk 3

acquire the basic skills necessary for a professional artist."[3] Although it was "difficult for women to become artists during this time . . . [Gentileschi] was able to gain access to a world that would normally have been forbidden."[4]

Her father, Orazio, one of the first followers of Caravaggio, trained Gentileschi from an early age, but he recognized his limits as a teacher when her talent surpassed his. Orazio hired Agostino Tassi to tutor her in perspective, but the perspective Tassi imparted to Gentileschi had nothing to do with any artistic technique. During one of his "lessons," Tassi raped her, and continued sexual relations with promises of marriage. However, when it became apparent that Tassi had no intention of marrying Gentileschi, Orazio sued Tassi for ruining her honour.[5]

During the early 17th century, as Spear notes:

> legal and social dimensions of violent rape centred on questions of family and marriageability, in which women resembled (male) property for exchange . . . usually poor girls sought not the rapist's imprisonment, but either his hand in marriage or payment of a dowry . . . . Marriage, it must be emphasized, rather than rape, was the core substance of the litigation.[6]

Long quotations are indented four spaces.

[3]Wendy Slatkin, *Women Artists in History: From Antiquity to the Present* (Toronto: Prentice-Hall Canada, 1990), 49.

[4]Rebecca Corbell and Samantha Guy, "Artemisia Gentileschi and the Age of Baroque," 1995, <http://rubens.anu.edu.au/student.projects/artemisia/Artemisia.html> (25 February 2001).

[5]Slatkin, 49.

[6]Richard Spear, "Artemisia Gentileschi: Ten Years of Fact and Fiction," *Art Bulletin* 82 (September 2000): 570.

Note that the reference to Corbell and Guy does not have a page number because it is an Internet source (see pages 102–105).

12g

Senyk 4

Gentileschi, as an unmarried woman, was classified as "damaged property." She was subjected to torture, a humiliating public trial, and a medical examination to prove that she was a virgin before the rape.[7] The sexual assaults, compounded by the ordeal of the trial, no doubt caused a "crystallizing moment of recognition of sexuality and gender power" in Gentileschi.[8]

The emotional chaos resulting from the assaults and the trial is most likely expressed in Gentileschi's work, *Judith Decapitating Holofernes*, painted shortly after the trial was dismissed.[9] Gentileschi's interpretation of this biblical story is particularly gruesome; she uses vivid colours, indicating strong, vehement emotion and enhancing the sense of violence and movement.[10] This painting is clearly a "cathartic expression of the artist's private, and perhaps repressed, rage."[11] Rebecca Corbell and Samantha Guy suggest that "the violence her Judith wreaks on Holofernes is strongly suggestive of the turmoil she must have been experiencing."[12]

Caravaggio also depicts this scene in his *Judith and Holofernes*. Both artists depict the moment when Judith severs Holofernes' head, but Caravaggio positions the figures across the picture surface, weakening the overall effect; the characters seem less active in decapitating Holofernes and more like passive witnesses. Gentileschi, instead, chooses to intersect the arms of all three figures in the centre of the picture plane, "fixing the viewer's attention inescapably on the

[7]Corbell and Guy.

[8]Griselda Pollock, review of *Artemisia Gentileschi: The Image of the Female Hero in Italian Baroque Art*, by Mary Garrard, *Art Bulletin* 72 (September 1990): 503.

[9]Corbell and Guy.

[10]Ibid.

[11]Spear, 569.

[12]Corbell and Guy.

Footnotes are separated from the text by triple spacing. Items in footnotes are separated by commas for author, work, and publication data.

12g

grisly act much more convincing[ly] than Caravaggio."[13] Caravaggio depicts Judith as a weak, ineffective female, drawing back distastefully, almost cringing at the sight of blood, whereas Gentileschi's Judith looks "as if she is [angrily] struggling to pull the sword through Holofernes' [neck]."[14] Perhaps Gentileschi is expressing the anger she feels about her helplessness and vulnerability as a woman.

[A portion of this paper has been omitted]

With a new perspective on the world after the experiences of the sexual assaults and the charade of a trial, Artemisia Gentileschi went on to develop her unique style combining dynamic, gruesome naturalism with innovative interpretations of typical Renaissance and Baroque themes. "She adapted some of Caravaggio's devices to forge an original style of strength and beauty. She expressed her identity as a woman and as an artist."[15] As a woman, Gentileschi identified with the plight of the heroine, whereas her male colleagues identified with the villain's anticipated pleasure.

Artemisia Gentileschi's great contribution to art is found in the "categorically different treatment of major themes around the well-established topos of the heroic woman." [16] Because most artists and patrons have historically been men, naturally most paintings would represent the perspective of the male; and as Garrard notes, ". . . [men have been] drawn by instinct to identify more with the villain than with the heroine."[17]

Katrina now advances her conclusion. See pages 82–83 for details.

---

[13]Slatkin, 51.
[14]Corbell and Guy.
[15]Slatkin, 54.
[16]Pollock, 50.
[17]Garrard, 194.

12g

Senyk 6

As a result of her experiences, Gentileschi began to reinterpret traditional themes from the viewpoint of the dynamic, assertive female protagonist. In her television documentary, "Artemisia," Adrienne Clarkson asserts that this artist "(broke) the constraints of her female condition to become arguably the most remarkable woman painter of the post-modern period."[18] Through her body of work, Gentileschi explores in depth women's demands to be justly represented.

[18]Adrienne Clarkson, "Artemisia," *Adrienne Clarkson Presents* (Toronto: CBC-TV, 25 January 1993).

12g

The references
(Works Cited)
go on a
separate page.

Katrina's
bibliography
demonstrates
the citation
form for books,
journal articles,
an Internet
source, and a
television
program.

Works Cited

Clarkson, Adrienne. "Artemisia." *Adrienne Clarkson Presents*. Toronto: CBC-TV, 25 January 1993.

Corbell, Rebecca, and Samantha Guy. "Artemisia Gentileschi and the Age of Baroque." <http://rubens.anu.edu.au/student.projects/artemisia/Artemisia.html> (25 February 2001).

Garrard, Mary. Artemisia Gentileschi: The Image of the Female Hero in Italian Baroque Art. Princeton: Princeton UP, 1989.

Hergenhahn, B. R., and Matthew H. Olson. *An Introduction to Theories of Personality*. 5th ed. Toronto: Prentice Hall Canada, 1999.

Pollock, Griselda. Review Artemisia Gentileschi: The Image of the Female Hero in Italian Baroque Art, by Mary Garrard. *Art Bulletin* 72 (September 1990): 499–505.

Slatkin, Wendy. *Women Artists in History: From Antiquity to the Present*. Toronto: Prentice-Hall Canada, 1990. 49–54.

Spear, Richard. "Artemisia Gentileschi: Ten Years of Fact and Fiction." *Art Bulletin* 82 (September 2000): 568–579.

12g

Appendix

Glossary of Manuscript Style

The alphabetical glossary that follows will answer most of your miscellaneous questions about matters of form, such as margins, pagination, dates, and numbers. For matters not addressed below, consult the index, which will direct you to appropriate pages elsewhere in this text.

Abbreviations

Employ abbreviations often and consistently in notes and citations, but do not use them within sentences in the text.

Abbreviations for Technical Terms

abr.	abridged
AD or CE	*anno Domini* ("in the year of the Lord") precedes numerals, no space between letters, as in "AD 350"; "of the Common Era" follows numerals, as in "350 CE"
anon.	anonymous
art., arts.	article(s)
assn.	association
BC or BCE	"before Christ" or "before the Common Era" follow numerals with no space between letters, as in "500 BC"
ca., c.	*circa* ("about"); used to indicate an approximate date, as in "ca. 1812"
cf.	*confer* ("compare") one source with another); however, not to be used in place of "see" or "see also"
ch., chs.	chapter(s); also shown as chap., chaps.
comp.	compiled by or compiler
diss.	dissertation
doc.	document
ed., eds.	editor(s), edition, or edited by
e.g.	*exempli gratia* ("for example"); preceded and followed by a comma
esp.	especially, as in "312–15, esp. 313"
et al.	*et alii* ("and others"); "John Smith et al." means John Smith and other authors
etc.	*et cetera* ("and so forth")
f., ff.	page or pages following a given page; "8f." means page eight and the following page; "ff" means following pages

ibid.	*ibidem* ("in the same place"); i.e., in the immediately preceding title; normally capitalized and underlined as in "<u>Ibid</u>., p. 34"
i.e.	*id est* ("that is"); preceded and followed by a comma
ms., mss.	manuscript(s), as in "(Cf. the ms. of Ford)"
n, nn	note(s), as "23, n 2" or "51 n"
n.d.	no date (in a book's title or copyright pages)
no., nos.	number(s)
pt., pts.	part(s)
rev.	revised, revised by, revision, review, or reviewed
rpt.	reprint, reprinted
sec(s).	section(s)
ser.	series
sic	"thus"; placed in brackets to indicate an error has been made in the quoted passage and the writer is quoting accurately; see example on page 94
st., sts.	stanza(s)
trans., tr.	translator, translated, translated by, or translation
ts., tss.	typescript, typescripts
vol., vols.	volume(s); e.g., vol. 3
vs., v.	versus ("against"); used in citing legal cases

Abbreviation of Publishers' Names

In your bibliography entries, use a shortened form of a publisher's name: ALA for the American Library Association; Wilfrid Laurier UP for Wilfrid Laurier University Press; and Pearson for Pearson Education Canada.

Abbreviation of Biblical Works

Use parenthetical documentation for biblical references in the text by placing the entry within parentheses immediately after the quotation, for example (Gen. 9.11). Do not italicize or underline titles of books of the Bible. Abbreviate books of the Bible except some very short titles, such as Ezra and Mark. Here are examples:

1 and 2 Chron.
Deut.

Abbreviations for Literary Works

In parenthetical documentation, use underlined or italicized abbreviations for titles of plays, novels, and other major works once the title is established. A reference to page 18 of Kogawa's *Obasan* could appear as (*Oba.* 18). Here are a few additional examples that show how to use a key word, the initial letters, or an abbreviation followed by a period:

Ado	*Much Ado about Nothing*
CT	*The Canterbury Tales*
Beo.	*Beowulf*

Ampersand

Avoid using the ampersand symbol (&) unless custom demands it (e.g., "A&P"). In MLA, CBE, and CMS styles, use "and" for in-text citations (e.g., Smith and Jones 213–14). In APA style use "&" within parenthetical citations: (Spenser & Wilson, 1994, p. 73). Use "and" within the text of APA papers: (Spenser and Wilson found the results in error.).

Arabic Numerals

Both the MLA style and the APA style require Arabic numerals for volumes, books, parts, and chapters of works; acts, scenes, and lines of plays; cantos, stanzas, and lines of poetry.

Spell out whole numbers from one through nine. Write as Arabic numerals all numbers 10 and above (such as 23, 154, 1269). Write as Arabic numerals any numbers below 10 that cannot be spelled out in one or two words (e.g., $3^1/4$ or 6.234).

For inclusive numbers that indicate a range, give the second number in full for numbers through 99 (e.g., 3–5, 15–21, 70–96). In MLA style, with three digits or more, give only the last two digits in the second number unless more are needed for clarity (e.g., 98–101, 110–12, 989–1001, 1030–33, 2766–854). In APA style, with three digits or more, give all numbers (e.g., 110–112, 1030–1033, 2766–2854).

Numbers Expressed As Figures in Your Text

Use figures in your text according to the following examples:

- All numbers 10 and above
  the subjects who were 25 years old (*but* a twenty-five-year-old woman)
  several parking lots with 468 spaces
- Numbers that represent ages, dates, time, size, score, amounts of money, and numerals used as numerals
  Ages 6 through 14
  AD 200 *but* 200 BC
  in 1991–92 *or* from 1991 to 1992, *but not* from 1991–92
  32–34 *or* pages 32–34, *but not* pp. 32–34
  lines 32–34 *but not* ll. 32–34
  March 5, 1991, *or* 5 March 1991, *but not* both styles
  1990s *or* the nineties
  six o'clock *or* 6:00 p.m.
  6% *but* use "six percent" in discussions with few numbers
  $9.00 or $9
  scores in the 92–96 percentile
  from 1965 through 1970
- Statistical and mathematical numbers
  6.213
  0.5 *but not* .5
  consumed exactly 0.45 of the fuel

- Numbers that precede units of measurement
  a 5-milligram tablet
  use 7 centimetres of this fluid
- Numbers below 10 grouped with higher numbers
  3 out of 14 subjects
  units 8, 12, and 256
  but 15 tests in three categories (Tests and categories are different groups; they are not being compared.)

Numbers Expressed As Words in Your Text

Spell out numbers in the following instances:

- Numbers less than 10 that are not used as measurements
  three students
  he is one who should know
  a group of six professors
- Numbers less than 10 that are grouped with other numbers below 10
  five sessions with six examinations in each session
  the fifth of eight participants
- Common fractions
  one fifth of the student population
- Any number that begins a sentence
  Thirty participants elected to withdraw.
- The numbers *zero* and *one* when used alone
  zero-base budget planning
  a one-line paragraph
  one response *but* 1 of 15 responses

Numbers As Both Words and Figures

Combine words and figures in these situations:

- Back-to-back modifiers
  twelve 6-year-olds or 12 six-year-olds, *but not* 12 6-year olds
- Large numbers
  an operating budget of $4 million

Numbers in Documentation

Use numbers with in-text citations and Works Cited or Reference entries according to the following examples:

(*Ham.* 5.3.16–18)
(*Faust* 2.140)
(2 Sam. 2.1–8)
(Fredericks 23–24) (MLA style)
(Fredericks, 1995, pp. 23–24) (APA and CBE style)
2 vols.
Rpt. as vols. 13 and 14

MS CCCC 210
16 mm., 29 min., colour
Monograph 1962–M2

Asterisks

Do not use asterisks (*) to indicate tables, content notes, or illustrations. Use numbers for tables and figures (e.g., Table 2 or Figure 3) and use letters for content notes.

Borders

Use a border, with restraint, for graphs, charts, highlighted text, and other material that deserves special emphasis.

Bullets and Numbers for Lists

Computers supply several bullet and number formats (circle, square, diamond, triangle, number, letter) for lists:

* Observation 1: Kindergarten class
* Observation 2: Grade 1 class
* Observation 3: Grade 2 class

Capitalization

Capitalize after a Colon

When a *complete* sentence follows a colon, MLA style does *not* capitalize the first word.

The consequences of this decision will be disastrous: each division of the corporation will be required to cut 20 percent of its budget.

The APA style *does* capitalize the first word after the colon when a complete sentence follows.

They have agreed on the outcome: Informed subjects perform better than do uninformed subjects.

Capitalize Proper Names

Capitalize proper names used as adjectives *but not* the words used with them: Einstein's theory, Salk's vaccine.

Capitalize Some Compound Words

Capitalize the second part of a hyphenated compound word only when it is used in a heading with other capitalized words:

Low-Frequency Sound Equipment

but

Low-frequency sound distortion is caused by several factors

Capitalize Specific Departments or Courses

Capitalize the specific departments or courses, but use lowercase when they are used in a general sense: "Department of Psychology" *but* "the psychology department."

Capitalize Some Titles

For books, journals, magazines, and newspapers capitalize the first word, the last word, and all principal words, including words that follow hyphens in compound terms (e.g., French-Speaking Islands). *Note:* Computer printouts often do not capitalize important words in titles; however, you should follow capitalization rules even in those cases. Do not capitalize the articles *a, an,* and *the,* prepositions that introduce phrases, conjunctions, and the *to* in infinitives when these words occur in the middle of the title (e.g., *The Loved and the Lost*). For titles of articles and parts of books, capitalize as for books (e.g., "Writing the Final Draft" or "Appendix 2"). If the first line of the poem serves as the title, reproduce it exactly as it appears in print (anyone lived in a pretty how town).

Note that some scholarly styles, such as APA, capitalize only the first word and proper names of reference titles (including the first word of subtitles). Study the appropriate style for your field as found in Chapters 9, 10, 11, and 12.

Content Endnotes

As a general rule, put important matters in your text. Use a content note to explain research problems, conflicts in the testimony of the experts, matters of importance that are not germane to your discussion, interesting tidbits, credit to people and sources not mentioned in the text, and other tangential matters that you think will interest the readers. Content notes should conform to these rules:

- Content notes are *not* documentation notes. Use in-text citations, not content notes, to document your sources.
- Content notes should be placed on a separate page(s) following the last page of text. Do not write them as footnotes at the bottom of pages.
- At a computer, use a word processing code to produce superscript numbers (e.g., [1]). The computer superscript numerals often appear in a smaller size and a different font. Each superscript numeral should follow the material to which it refers, usually at the end of a sentence, with no space between the superscript numeral and a word or mark of punctuation, as shown in this example:

  > Third, a program to advise university students about politically correct language and campus attitudes[1] may incite demonstrations by both faculty and students against the censorship of free speech.

- Sources mentioned in endnotes must appear on your "Works Cited" page even if they are not mentioned in the main body of text.

The samples below demonstrate content notes.

Related Matters Not Germane to the Text

[1]The problems of politically correct language are explored in Adams, and Tucker (4–5). These authorities cite the need for caution by administrators who would impose new measures on speech and behaviour.

Blanket Citation

[2]On this point see Giarrett (3–4), de Young (579), and Kinard (405–07).

[3]Cf. Campbell (<u>Masks</u> 1: 170–225; <u>Hero</u> 342–45), and Baird (300–44).

Other content notes can be used to show

- a major source requiring frequent in-text citations
- a reference to source materials
- an explanation of tools, methods, or testing procedures
- statistics
- acknowledgments for assistance or support
- variables or conflicts in the evidence
- literature on a related topic

Copyright Law

"Fair use" of the materials of others is permitted without the need for specific permission as long as your purpose is non-commercial criticism, scholarship, or research. Under those circumstances, you can quote from sources and reproduce artistic works within reasonable limits.

To protect your work, type in the upper right-hand corner of your manuscript, "Copyright © 20_____ by _____." Fill the blanks with the proper year and your name. Then, to register the work, contact the Canadian Intellectual Property Office (CIPO) in Hull, Quebec (see **http://cipo.gc.ca/**).

Covers and Binders

Most instructors prefer that you submit manuscript pages with one staple in the upper left corner. Do not use a cover or binder unless the instructor requires one.

Dates

See "Arabic Numerals" pages 165–167.

Figures and Tables

A table is a systematic presentation of materials, usually in columns. A figure is any item that is not a table: a blueprint, chart, diagram, drawing, graph, photo, photostat, map, and so on. Label figures below the art, but label tables above. Remember to indicate the source of the material in figures and tables.

Here are samples:

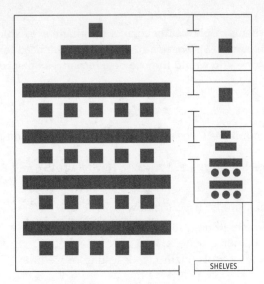

Figure 1: Computer Laboratory with Private
Work Rooms and a Small Group Room.

Table 1
Student Response by Year on Nuclear Energy Policy

	1st	2nd	3rd	4th
1. More nuclear power	150	301	75	120
2. Less nuclear power	195	137	111	203
3. Present policy is acceptable	87	104	229	37

Fonts

Most computers offer a variety of typefaces. Courier (`Courier`), the type-writer font, is always a safe choice, but you may use others, such as a non-serif typeface like Arial (**Arial**) or a serif typeface like Times Roman (**Times Roman**). Use the same font consistently throughout your text, but shift to different fonts if desired for tables, illustrations, and other matter.

Foreign Cities

In general, spell the names of foreign cities as they are written in original sources. However, for purposes of clarity, you may substitute an English name or provide both with one name in parentheses:

Köln (Cologne)   Praha (Prague)

Foreign Languages

Underline or italicize foreign words used in an English text:

Like his friend Olaf, he is <u>aut Caesar, aut nihil</u>, either overpowering perfection or ruin and destruction.

Do not underline or italicize quotations of a foreign language:

Obviously, he uses it to exploit, in the words of Jean Laumon, "une admirable mine de thèmes poétiques."

Do not underline or italicize foreign titles of magazine or journal articles, but do underline or italicize the names of the magazines or journals:

Arrigoitia, Luis de. "Machismo, folklore y creación en Mario Vargas Llosa." <u>Sin nombre</u> 13.4 (1983): 19–25.

Do not underline or italicize foreign words of places, institutions, proper names, or titles that precede proper names:

Racine became extremely fond of Mlle Champmeslé, who interpreted his works at the Hotel de Bourgogne.

For titles of French, Italian, Spanish, and Latin works, capitalize the first word and proper nouns, but not adjectives derived from proper nouns:

<u>La noche de Tlatelolco: Testimonios de historia oral</u>
<u>Realismo y realidad en la narrativa argentina</u>

For titles of German works, capitalize the first word, all nouns, and all adjectives derived from names of persons, such as "Homerian":

<u>Über die Religion: Reden an die Gebildeten unter ihren Verächtern</u>

Headings

Begin every *major* heading on a new page of your paper (title page, opening page, notes, appendix, works cited or references). Centre the heading in capital and lower case letters (e.g., Appendix) one inch from the top of the sheet. Use a double space between the heading and your first line of text. Number *all* text pages, including those with major headings. Use the following guideline for writing subheads in your paper.

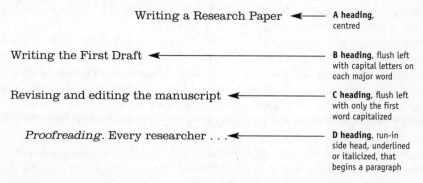

Writing a Research Paper ⟵ **A heading,** centred

Writing the First Draft ⟵ **B heading,** flush left with capital letters on each major word

Revising and editing the manuscript ⟵ **C heading,** flush left with only the first word capitalized

Proofreading. Every researcher . . . ⟵ **D heading,** run-in side head, underlined or italicized, that begins a paragraph

Hyphenation

Do not hyphenate words at the end of lines. If necessary, turn off your computer's automatic hyphenation command.

Indentation

Indent paragraphs five spaces or one half inch. In MLA style, indent long quotations of four or more lines 10 spaces or one inch from the left margin. In other styles, indent long quotations five spaces. Hanging indentations for bibliography entries are five spaces.

Italics

If your word-processing system and your printer will reproduce italic lettering, use it. Otherwise, show italics in a typed manuscript by underlining (see also "Underlining," page 175).

Margins

A basic one-inch margin on all sides is recommended. Place your page number one-half inch down from the top edge of the paper and one inch from the right edge. Your software will provide a ruler, menu, or style palette that allows you to set the margins. *Note:* If you develop a header, the running head may appear one inch from the top, in which case your first line of text will begin one and one-half inches from the top.

Monetary Units

Spell out monetary amounts only if you can do so in no more than two words. Conform to the following:

$10 *or* ten dollars
$14.25 *but not* fourteen dollars and twenty-five cents
$4 billion *or* four billion dollars
$10.3 billion *or* $10 300 000 000

In business and technical writing that frequently uses numbers, use numerals with appropriate symbols: $99.45; 6 @ $15.00; £92.

Names of Persons

As a rule, the first time that you mention a person use the full name (e.g., Ernest Hemingway, Margaret Atwood) and thereafter use only the surname, such as Hemingway or Atwood. *Note:* The MLA and CMS footnote styles conform to these instructions, but APA style and CBE style use *only* last names in all cases in the text. Omit formal titles (e.g., Mr., Mrs., Dr., Hon.) in textual and note references to distinguished persons. Convention suggests that certain prominent figures require the title (e.g., Lord Byron, Dr. Johnson, Dame Edith Sitwell) while others, for no apparent reason, do not (e.g., Tennyson, Browne, and Hillary rather than Lord Tennyson, Sir Thomas Browne, or Sir Edmund Hillary). Where custom dictates, you may employ simplified names of famous persons (e.g., use Dante rather than the surname Alighieri and use Michelangelo rather than Michelangelo Buonarroti). You may also use pseudonyms where custom dictates (e.g., George Eliot, Mark Twain). Refer to fictional characters by names used in the fictional work (e.g., Huck, Lord Jim, Agaguk, Capt. Ahab).

Numbering Pages

Use a running head to number your pages in the upper right corner of the page. Depending on the software, you can create the head with the "numbering" or the "header" feature.

Use lower case Roman numerals (ii, iii, iv) on any pages that precede your text. If you have a separate title page, count it as page 1 but do not type it on the page. You *should* put a page number on your opening page of text, even if you include course identification (see page 110).

Numbering a Series of Items

Within a sentence, incorporate a series of items with parenthetical numbers or lower case letters: University instructors are usually divided into four ranks: (1) instructors, (2) assistant professors, (3) associate professors, (4) full professors. Present a longer group of items in indented columns with bullet or numbers. However, avoid point form in academic papers.

Percentages

In discussions with infrequent use of numbers, spell out percentages when they can be spelled out in one or two words:

percent *not* per cent
nine percent *but* 150 percent
a two-point average *but* a 2.5 average
one tonne *but* 0.907 tonne or 3.150 tonnes
forty-five percent *but* 45^1/$_2$ percent *or* 45^1/$_2$%

In business, scientific, and technical writing that requires frequent use of percentages, write all percentages as numerals with appropriate symbols: 100%, 45^1/$_2$, 12%.

Roman Numerals

Use capital Roman numerals for titles of persons (Elizabeth II) and major sections of an outline (see pages 41–42). Use lower case Roman numerals for preliminary pages of text, as for a preface or introduction (iii, iv, v). Otherwise, use Arabic numerals (e.g., Vol. 5, Act 2, Ch. 16, Plate 32, 2 Sam. 2.1–8, or *Iliad* 2.121–30); however, when writing for some instructors in history, philosophy, religion, music, art, and theatre, you may need to use Roman numerals (e.g., III, Act II, I Sam. ii.1–8, *Hamlet* I.ii.5–6).

Running Heads

In MLA style repeat your last name in the upper right corner of every page just in front of the page number (see "Numbering Pages" above). The APA style requires a short title, instead of your name, preceding the page number at the top of each page (see pages 129–130). For Chicago footnote and CBE number styles, follow your instructor's directions. See the sample papers in Chapters 9, 10, 11, and 12.

Spacing

As a general rule, double space everything—the body of the paper, all indented quotations, and all reference entries. Footnotes and endnotes, if used, should be single spaced, but double spacing should be used between each entry (see pages 150–154). Space after punctuation according to these stipulations:

- Use one space after commas, semicolons, and colons.
- Use one space after periods and other punctuation marks at the end of sentences.
- Use no space after periods that separate parts of a reference citation (*Ham.* 3.2.4–7).
- Do not use a space before or after periods within abbreviations (i.e., e.g., a.m.).
- Use one space between initials of personal names (M. C. Boone).
- Do not use a space before or after a hyphen (a three-part test) *but* use one space before and after a hyphen used as a minus sign (e.g., a – b + c) and one space before but none after a hyphen for a negative value (e.g., –3.25).
- Do not use a space before or after a dash (the evidence—interviews and statistics—was published).

Table of Contents

A table of contents is usually unnecessary for undergraduate research papers, but do check with your instructor.

Titles

Shortened Titles in the Text

In MLA style use abbreviated titles of books and articles mentioned often in the text after a first, full reference. Mention <u>The Handmaid's Tale</u> and thereafter use <u>Handmaid's</u>. Be certain to underline or italicize it when referring to the work.

Titles within Titles

For a title to a book that includes another title indicated by quotation marks, retain the quotation marks.

<u>O. Henry's Irony in "The Gift of the Magi"</u>

For a title of an article within quotation marks that includes a title to a book, as indicated by underlining, retain the underlining or use italic lettering.

"<u>Great Expectations</u> as a Novel of Initiation"

When a title of an article in quotation marks includes a second title, single quotation marks should be used to enclose the second title.

"A Reading of Theriault's 'Agaguk'"

For an underlined title to a book that incorporates another title that normally receives underscoring, do not underline or italicize the shorter title nor place it within quotation marks.

<u>Using Shakespeare's</u> Romeo and Juliet <u>in the Classroom</u>

Underlining

Underlining Titles of Works

Underline or italicize the titles of the following types of works:

Type of Work	Example
ballet	*The Nutcracker*
book	*More Canada Firsts*
bulletin	*Production Memo 3*
film	*The English Patient*
journal	*Canadian Journal of Sociology*
magazine	*Maclean's*
newspaper	*The Globe and Mail*
novel	*Obasan*
opera	*Rigoletto*
painting	*Mona Lisa*
pamphlet	*Ten Goals for Successful Sales*
periodical	*Canadian Theatre Review*
play	*The Rez Sisters*
radio show	*As It Happens*
recording	*The Poems of E. Pauline Johnson*
sculpture	*David*
ship	*Titanic*
symphony	Beethoven's *Eroica* (but Beethoven's Symphony no. 3 in E-flat to identify form, number, and key)
television	*Hockey Night in Canada* (program title, not a single episode)

In contrast, place quotation marks around the titles of articles, essays, chapters, sections, short poems, stories, songs, lectures, sermons, reports, and individual episodes of television programs.

If separately published as a single book or booklet, underline titles of essays, lectures, poems, proceedings, reports, sermons, and stories. However, these items are usually published as an anthology of sermons or a collection of stories, in which case you would underscore the title of the anthology or collection.

Do not italicize or underline sacred writings (Genesis or Old Testament); series (The New American Nation Series); editions (Variorum Edition of W. B. Yeats); societies (Canadian Humane Society); courses (Greek Mythology); divisions of a work (preface, appendix, canto 3, scene 2); or descriptive phrases (Trudeau's farewell address).

Underlining Individual Words for Emphasis

Underline or italicize a word used as a word:

> The new word <u>hood</u> gives special meaning to its parent, <u>neighbourhood</u>.

Some special words and symbols require italics or underlining:

- Species, genera, and varieties:

  > *Penstemon caespitosus subsp. thompsoniae*

- Letter, word, or phrase cited as a linguistic sample:

  > the letter *e* in the word *let*

- Letter used as statistical symbol and algebraic variable:

  > trial n of the t test or C (3, 14) = 9.432

Word Division

If possible, avoid dividing any word at the end of a line. Leave the line short rather than divide a word (see "Hyphenation").

Credits

Index

Citing an Internet Article

QUICK REFERENCE

APA Style

Bowman, M. L. (2000). The diversity of diversity: Canadian-American differences and their implications for clinical training and APA accreditation. (Abstract). *Canadian Psychology, 41.4.* Retrieved May 12, 2001, from www.cpa.ca/cp/tc-cpnov00.html

CBE Style

Canadian Medical Association. Natural health products: Ensuring safety, quality and efficacy. 2000. Available from www.cma.ca/advocacy/political/2000/09-29.htm. Accessed 2002 Apr 22.

CMS Style

GaoYi, "French Revolutionary Studies in Today's China," *Canadian Journal of History* 32 (1997) <www.usask.ca/history/cjh> (14 February 2002).

MLA Style

Kilbourn, Russell. "Re-Writing 'Reality': Reading *The Matrix.*" *Canadian Journal of Film Studies 9* (2000). Abstract. 5 July 2001 <www.film.queensu.ca/FSAC/CJFS.html>.

Common Proofreading Symbols

i   error in spelling (mistake) with correction in margin

lc   lowercase (misTake)

⌒   close up (mis take)

I   delete and close up (misstake)

⊢—⫽   delete and close up more than one letter
(the/mistakes and/errors continue)

∧   insert (mitake)

tr   transpose elements (theif)

⌒◯   material to be corrected or moved, with instructions
in the margin, or material to be spelled out (corp)

caps or ≡   capitalize (Huck finn and Tom Sawyer)

¶   insert paragraph

e   delete (a mistakes)

add space

⊙   period

⌃;   comma

⌃;   semicolon

∨   apostrophe or single closing quotation mark

∨   single opening quotation mark

∨∨   double quotation marks

bf   boldface

stet   let stand as it is; ignore marks